BECOMING a
LEARNING
TEAM

A guide to a teacher-led cycle of
continuous improvement

SECOND EDITION

Stephanie Hirsh
and
Tracy Crow

learningforward
THE PROFESSIONAL LEARNING ASSOCIATION

THE PROFESSIONAL LEARNING ASSOCIATION

Learning Forward
504 S. Locust St.
Oxford, OH 45056
800-727-7288
Fax: 513-523-0638
Email: office@learningforward.org
www.learningforward.org

Becoming a Learning Team: A Guide to a Teacher-led Cycle of Continuous Improvement, Second Edition
Stephanie Hirsh and Tracy Crow

Editor: Joyce Pollard
Designer: Jane Thurmond

© Learning Forward, 2018.

Requests for permission to reprint or copy portions of this book for other purposes must be submitted to Christy Colclasure by fax (513-523-0638) or email (christy.colclasure@learningforward.org). All requests must specify the number of copies that will be made and how the material will be used. Please allow two weeks for a response.

Printed in the United States of America.

Item: B611

ISBN: 978-0-9903158-8-9

Contents

Online tools

All tools can be found online at http://learningforward.org/publications/learning-team-tools. For access, use password **TeamCycle17**.

Acknowledgments

earning Forward's position is that school-based professional learning is the most effective process for ensuring that adult learning affects student learning positively. As Joellen Killion states in *Becoming a Learning School,* "The concept of school-based professional development recognizes that the school is the primary center of learning and that teachers can often learn best with and from one another" (2009, p. 8).

We also realize that schools exist within systems and systems play a fundamental role in promoting learning at the school. In fact, Learning Forward embraced that reality to write and publish *Becoming a Learning System,* which allowed us to present Learning Forward's vision of district leaders' roles in such systems. *Becoming a Learning School* and *Becoming a Learning System* have inspired many educators to develop learning schools and systems. Both of these books have been used successfully throughout the country and internationally to help educators develop purposeful, effective learning organizations.

A logical next step is the creation of *Becoming a Learning Team.* This latest entry in Learning Forward's "learning" series focuses on the actions of the professional learning team in the application of a cycle of continuous learning. Much has been written about professional learning communities and learning cycles. When preparing to write this book, we were surprised to find that we, and other Learning Forward authors,

had written about several learning cycles with varying stages and levels of complexity. We soon realized that the earlier publications focus on cycles of continuous improvement for broader systems. So, those very efforts along with the varied experiences of school teams engaged with learning cycles, inspired our focus of this book: the teacher learning team. The five-stage team learning cycle described in these pages offers teacher teams the steps toward intentional, collaborative professional learning.

We believe that if appropriately applied, the ideas and actions promoted in *Becoming a Learning Team* will result in teachers experiencing and modeling high-quality professional learning — professional learning that is long term, sustained, and standards driven; grounded in a cycle of continuous improvement; and capable of inspiring all to take responsibility for the learning of every adult and student in the school.

We are grateful to the district, provincial, and school-based educators who shared their stories, accomplishments, and setbacks as they continue to leverage learning teams to address critical student learning challenges. We appreciate their courage to do that work and their willingness to share what they are learning so that we may continue to promote the professional learning team cycle as a job-embedded strategy that can lead improved teaching and learning for all students. We thank: Clara Howitt, Greater

Essex County District School Board, Windsor, Ontario; Gina Cash, Elkridge Landing Middle School, Elkridge, Maryland and Brenda J. Conley, Towson University, Towson, Maryland; Tanya Batzel and Kellie Randall, Cherry Creek School District, Centennial, Colorado; Dwayne A. Young, Kelly H. Baugh, Amy Carey, and Gretchen Polivka, Centreville Elementary, Centreville Virginia; Leslie Ceballos, Dallas, Texas; Samuel Milder and Natalie Pennington, New York City Department of Education.

We are indebted to Joyce Pollard and Jane Thurmond, our production team who worked along with us as we studied, thought, talked, wrote and rewrote chapters, tools, figures throughout the development of this book. As production editor Joyce also worked with the six author teams to create vignettes that display clarity and consistency, yet honor the widely varying conditions in which professional learning teams learn and work. Jane Thurmond, graphic designer extraordinaire, deserves praise and our thanks for her careful consideration of every aspect of production, her flexibility and responsiveness, and her constant attention to the smallest details, all of which are critical to creating a quality final product.

We also want to thank our colleagues who generously gave us the benefit of their time and knowledge. Terry Morganti-Fisher and Anne Conzemius contributed to the discussion of goal setting and related learning tools. Terry gave Stephanie and Joyce hours of her time to listen and ask probing questions that helped clarify many of the ideas discussed in this book. We appreciate the comments and advice of Alexandra Fuentes, biology teacher, Alexandria, Virginia; Scott Thompson, Office of Instructional Practice, District of Columbia Public Schools, Washington, DC; and Jennifer M. Walker, supervisor of school improvement, Warren G. Harding High School, Warren, Ohio. We appreciate informal comments and ongoing support from Juliette Heinze, executive director, knowledge sharing, and Julie Leopold, executive director, continuous learning, New York City Department of Education.

We express our continual gratitude to Joellen Killion, senior advisor, Learning Forward, for her help and guidance. As always, Joellen was generous, kind, but candid. She tapped her deep reservoir of knowledge and experience to help straighten the strands of a complex and detailed learning team cycle process. As is the case with so many of our writing projects, the vision is clearer and the book more useful because of Joellen's contribution.

Finally, we acknowledge that this project, like all the work we do, could not be accomplished without the loving support of our families. Because they act as counselors and cheerleaders (as needed), find creative ways, as we work, to spend time with us (when possible), and shoulder many home responsibilities (with patience), we have been able to focus on the challenging task of writing. We love them and thank them for partnering with us in another endeavor.

Foreword

The Monarch Butterfly Test

The migration of monarch butterflies carries a lesson for professional learning that is captured in *Becoming a Learning Team: A Guide to a Teacher-led Cycle of Continuous Improvement.* The butterflies begin their annual journey south across the U.S. as schools and districts throughout the country roll out their professional development programs for teachers at the start of the school year. They return north in late spring and into the summer as educators wrap up and reflect on the school year.

The black and bright orange coloring of the monarch is easy to recognize. It is also easy to confuse with the similarly patterned viceroy butterfly. The difference is that the monarch contains cardenolide glycoside chemicals that make it poisonous. Birds, too, are fooled by the viceroy mimic. Once a bird has tasted the monarch, it will never eat either specie again even though the viceroy butterfly makes a tasty, nutritious meal. The bird simply cannot tell the butterflies apart.

Professional learning in education can also involve mimicry. It happens when we emulate some, but not all aspects of best practice. We spend money on programs that look great on paper, but do not result in the gains students need, not because they don't work, but because we mimic without full implementation. In *Becoming a Learning Team,* Stephanie Hirsh and Tracy Crow offer rich, clear guidance on how to build teams of teachers who continuously develop their professional expertise and improve outcomes for students.

In the seven years I taught high school biology, I was fortunate to work in schools that — by conventional standards — made heroic efforts to have job-embedded, quality professional learning rather than sporadic professional development events:

- We met in teams.
- We met for three to four hours each week.
- We looked at student data.
- We set learning goals.
- We observed teachers teach.

From an outsider's view, we had the makings of quality professional learning. As I read this book, I identified tools that would have enabled us to continuously refine our own professional learning and practice for greater impact on student learning.

Here are some ideas for ways to avoid educational mimicry:

1) **Dig deeply into many sources of student data to pinpoint students' learning needs. I**n one school, we graphed the number of students with A's, B's, C's and F's in the first quarter compared to the second and third quarter. Our aim was to use data on student grades to set goals and create an improvement plan. However, analysis of the number of students failing didn't explain *why* students were failing. *Becoming a Learning Team* recommends the use of multiple measures of student data to pinpoint the places where student understanding wanes, as well as who is struggling

and who is succeeding. Only then can educators create an informed plan for improving student learning.

2) **Identify key skills, attitudes, and behaviors that teachers apply in order to improve student learning.** In a previous teaching position, I saw that when students' reading scores were low, the administration provided training on close reading strategies. They used student data to develop learning goals for teachers. *Becoming a Learning Team* recommends that in addition to student data, teachers need data related to their own learning needs. This has several advantages. First, baseline data related to teacher skills in an identified area helps measure return on investment. With an established baseline it is possible to more accurately assess the impact professional learning has on teachers and students. Second, using teacher data facilitates differentiation and enables learning teams to tap into the expertise of colleagues.

3) **Prioritize and make effective use of collaborative learning time.** Peer observations are traditionally recognized as powerful learning experiences in teacher education. Just as a picture is worth a thousand words, seeing a peer in action is worth a thousand conversations. It's hard to imagine that strategy failing, but in my experience, it did, in part because the observation was disconnected from our professional goals. In *Becoming a Learning Team,* Hirsh and Crow recommend a coherent approach with a prioritized set of goals. At one school where I taught, we called this "strategic abandonment." This is not a simple thing to achieve because of the collaboration needed to accomplish it. In schools a million things need to be done and they can be done more efficiently when a team of teachers is in the same room. While it is tempting to coopt collaborative planning time for other projects, *Becoming a Learning Team* helps teams focus on how to make the best use of the collective time they have.

When I see the monarch at the beginning and end of each school year, I am reminded to learn from natures' examples of mimicry. For teacher professional learning that means working to distinguish effective professional learning team designs from those that mimic best practices.

The case studies, tools, and recommendations in *Becoming a Learning Team* can help teams of teachers engage in effective professional learning and avoid the pitfalls of mimicry.

— Alexandra Fuentes
Biology Teacher*

*The Foreword represents the author's personal views.

Introduction

Becoming a Learning Team is the most recent book in Learning Forward's series that includes *Becoming a Learning School* (NSDC, 2009) and *Becoming a Learning System* (Learning Forward, 2014). Building on the ideas presented in the series, this book deepens the details of Learning Forward's vision that every child attends a learning school in which they experience excellent teaching and learning every day.

For all students to attend great schools, we need both learning schools and learning systems. For several years, Learning Forward has advanced that belief through its research, publications, and resources. *Becoming a Learning Team* takes its place in the learning series to focus on the power of intentional, collaborative professional learning. This book envisions an ideal derived from research literature and real-life experience — the community of professionals who engage with one another in a cycle of continuous improvement to increase student learning.

At the core of the discussions throughout this book lie three ideas about learning:

- Teachers and leaders value a system of professional learning over sporadic instances of professional development.

- Collaborative learning is at the heart of a system of continuous learning.

- Teacher teams are intentional about their own learning.

Ideally, school and system leaders embrace continuous learning for all educators, including themselves. By taking such a stance, and all that it implies, they commit and contribute daily to a culture that puts learning first. In a system aligned with continuous learning focused on student outcomes, professional learning is the strategy driving improvement. Michael Fullan (2008)[1] uses systems language to describe the system of continuous improvement in which teachers' knowledge grows. He distinguishes between sporadic professional development, which he calls an input to a system of continuous learning, and the system of learning among teachers who are engaged every day in learning, teaching, monitoring, and refining to improve what they do in their classrooms and schools.

Much has been written about professional learning communities and cycles of continuous improvement or learning cycles. Chapter 2 discusses the history and span of learning cycles and what they have in common. Yet, the cycle that this five-stage learning

---

[1] Fullan, M. (2008). *The six secrets of change: What the best leaders do to help their organizations survive and thrive.* San Francisco, CA: Jossey-Bass.

team cycle represents is different. As discussed in Chapters 5 and 6, it drives forward from intentional, collaborative learning and improvement. Teams that apply this cycle will integrate curriculum, instructional materials, and intentional learning to ensure effective instruction for students. This book opens the door on a teacher team as the members learn and work collaboratively throughout the following five-stage learning team cycle:

- Analyze data: Examine student and educator learning challenges.
- Set goals: Identify shared goals for student and educator learning.
- Learn individually and collaboratively: Gain new knowledge and skills (e.g. content and content-specific pedagogy); examine assumptions, aspirations, and beliefs.
- Implement new learning: Implement lessons and assessments with deeper understanding and local support in the classroom.
- Monitor, assess, and adjust practice: Use evidence to assess and refine implementation and impact.

Learning Forward appreciates that teacher teams apply many different cycles in their schools and districts. Furthermore, not every school district will be at the same point in the learning journey, regardless of the cycle, so learners may begin by reviewing chapter titles to consider areas for attention.

Chapters 1–2 make the case for collaborative learning and the learning team cycle that promotes continuous improvement. Learners see how learning in community differs from collaborating or working together. They also get an overview of the learning team cycle.

Chapters 3–7 cover the five stages. These are the "procedural chapters" that allow readers and learners to shift between the big picture and the daily details to make sure they align with and address district,

school, student, team, and individual learning goals throughout each stage of the cycle.

- **Chapter 3, Analyze data.** By completing an in-depth process of data analysis teacher learning teams may begin identifying their most important student learning needs.
- **Chapter 4, Set goals.** Applying data analyses and identifying root causes for achievement gaps, teams craft learning goals for their students and plan intentionally for their own learning goals.
- **Chapter 5, Learn individually and collaboratively.** By surveying and digging deeply into curriculum units or modules, teachers determine learning priorities and means to address them. They apply new learning to practices or applicable lessons.
- **Chapter 6, Implement new learning.** By implementing their lessons and assessments with practice, reflection, and support from others, teams look forward to seeing their students attain better results.
- **Chapter 7, Monitor, assess, and adjust practice.** By monitoring new practices and assessing their impact on students, teams gain information to inform improvements in the future.

Chapters 8–9 help teams manage their work within the context of the bigger system, including how to stay on track in the face of challenges and create coherence across the system.

Chapter 10 addresses the roles of educators other than teachers in supporting school-based learning teams.

Structure of the chapters

Becoming a Learning Team shares structure and format with *Becoming a Learning School* and *Becoming a Learning System.* The three books are meant to

How to use *Becoming a Learning Team*

This book is designed to help multiple audiences.

Audience	Use
Teachers so they can . . .	• Learn in community as they accept collective responsibility for achievement of all students. • Effectively implement high-quality instructional materials and assessments. • Engage in or lead teacher learning teams in cycles of continuous improvement. • Plan intentionally for their own and student learning. • Exert their own agency in seeking support for their learning team cycles.
Master teachers (e.g. teacher leaders, coaches) so they can . . .	• Coach school learning teams in applying the five-stage learning cycle. • Facilitate school learning teams. • Build teachers' abilities, skills, and dispositions to move intentionally through a five-stage learning cycle.
Principals and school leaders so they can . . .	• Create a culture that supports teachers' continuous learning in community. • Model the attitudes and actions of a continuous learner. • Support the implementation of curriculum and assessment. • Expand teachers' access to resources such as research literature, time, data, and external partners. • Engage teachers in planning for and decision making about school-based learning teams.
District/Provincial professional learning leaders so they can . . .	• Lead and facilitate content-specific professional learning aligned with the Standards for Professional Learning. • Coach and support school leadership and learning teams in applying data-driven cycles of continuous improvement. • Integrate the district's efforts to implement high-quality curriculum with school-based, job-embedded learning.
District/Provincial leadership (e.g. area superintendents, assistant superintendents, principal supervisors) so they can . . .	• Ensure the district's vision and goals align with Learning Forward's definition of and Standards for Professional Learning. • Model standards-driven professional learning in their work with other district and school leaders. • Ensure that school leaders develop skills to support learning teams. • Provide sufficient resources to support teacher learning teams.
External partners (e.g. service centers, institutions of higher education, specialists, vendors) so they can . . .	• Support an organization focused on continuous learning. • Provide coaching, products, or services that support the stages of a team learning cycle. • Advise or provide research-based information related to the stages of a learning cycle.

be companion resources, and each addresses topics through the use of resources, case studies, and tools. Chapters begin and end with guiding questions to promote pre- and postassessments of users' commitment to deepening learning.

Readers will find these elements in each chapter:

- **Where we are.** These Likert-type statements allow readers to think about their school district's status and the chapter's key ideas. The statements may be used for pre- and postassessments.

- **Narrative.** The narrative builds foundational knowledge of the topic, offering ideas, practical examples, and research to promote deeper understanding, thoughtful actions, and ongoing reflection.

- **Vignettes.** Chapters 2–7 include vignettes written by educators working in districts, provinces, and schools across North America. Each story captures the experiences of members of a learning team at a point in time in their own learning cycle.

- **Reflections.** The questions in this section encourage readers to examine their commitment to creating learning teams. By reflecting on their own responses, readers can examine their thinking and consider how they will apply lessons learned.

- **Tools Index.** The Tools Index directs readers to accompanying online resources that will help teacher learning teams begin, facilitate, and reflect on their progression through the five-stage cycle.

These resources offer a starting point for applying school-based learning team cycles.

- **References.** Each chapter lists literature that teams for access and use to develop conceptual understanding, discover new protocols and practices, and stimulate creativity and innovation.

Creating the conditions in which teacher learning teams can function effectively is, by turns, a complex challenge and the simplest thing in the world. It is, after all, about learning, a basic human process. All people learn. Effective learning teams accept intentional, collaborative professional learning as an expectation for the team. They work to ensure that team members share both an intense moral belief in that expectation and a strong commitment to functioning as a learning team. They courageously implement the recommended strategies and continuously reflect on their progress toward their own and student learning goals.

Becoming a Learning Team sets out the expectations, standards, content, and actions that lead to effective school-based learning teams. It can be a resource to help teachers, teacher leaders, and school leaders better understand how to the definition and Standards for Professional Learning, review key roles and responsibilities, study essential structures, build cultures conducive to change and improvement, and find strategies and tools that will allow teachers learn collaboratively to achieve the district, school, team, and individual learning goals.

PART I

What does it mean to learn collaboratively?

CHAPTER 1

Collaboration is at the heart of learning

Where are we now?

Collaborative learning is central to the professional learning we experience in our school.

STRONGLY AGREE   AGREE   NO OPINION   DISAGREE   STRONGLY DISAGREE

In our school, we ensure that every teacher has access to collegial support to solve problems and build knowledge and skills.

STRONGLY AGREE   AGREE   NO OPINION   DISAGREE   STRONGLY DISAGREE

The implementation of collaborative learning in our school is supported by follow up from coaches, school leaders, and lead teachers.

STRONGLY AGREE   AGREE   NO OPINION   DISAGREE   STRONGLY DISAGREE

Collaborative learning in our school increases teacher self-efficacy and job satisfaction.

STRONGLY AGREE   AGREE   NO OPINION   DISAGREE   STRONGLY DISAGREE

Collaborative learning in our school appears to be related to increases in student and teacher learning.

STRONGLY AGREE   AGREE   NO OPINION   DISAGREE   STRONGLY DISAGREE

Our school provides time, learning, people, curriculum, and other resources to support effective collaborative learning.

STRONGLY AGREE   AGREE   NO OPINION   DISAGREE   STRONGLY DISAGREE

Overview

Teachers know what research continues to affirm: Their best resources for learning often are right next door. Yet, while innovative scheduling and schooling models offer a glimpse into new ways for teachers to work, many teachers continue to work in conditions characterized by isolation and lack of support, teacher turnover, and inconsistent teaching quality.

This chapter makes the case that teachers learning in community is an effective means of strengthening teaching and learning. The opening section describes conditions of teaching and learning that hinder the learning of adults in many schools. It follows with a discussion of seven elements that school leaders and teachers may employ to create a school culture of continuous improvement supportive of a cycle of collaborative learning. The chapter also points out an unrealistic expectation: Simply mandating teachers to learn and work together leads to their being able to do so. Empowering teacher teams to learn and solve problems together requires a vision of a certain way of knowing and working as well as an infrastructure that provides teams with leadership, resources, and support. Finally, this chapter includes a discussion of strategies that teachers can use on their own when their school cultures and conditions are less than favorable for collaborative learning.

How do systems transform the traditional model of teaching and learning?

Too many schools in the U.S. still send teachers into their classrooms with a stack of teaching materials and an invitation to emerge for occasional staff meetings and schoolwide professional development. Even with new college- and career-ready standards, conditions have not changed for many teachers. Only now their stack of materials is much higher with a set of standards perched on top and teaching materials that may or may not align with those standards. Hand in hand with the culture of isolation is the expectation that teachers, themselves, will handle the problems they encounter. While this expectation has been shifting somewhat, as more and more schools set aside time for professional learning communities, many teachers still find themselves alone with their teaching challenges, questions, and triumphs.

Researchers speculate about the role that such isolation might play on teacher effectiveness. Some evidence suggests that teacher performance plateaus at four years. That is, after new educators start in the profession, they show improvement in the first few years, but after four years they stay at the same level (Meyer, 2009). Researcher Jane Hannaway suggests that their working conditions may contribute to this flat lining of performance: "Teachers work in isolation. They learn what they learn and then they plateau. They get no valid input" (Meyer, 2009, para. 6).

Insufficient support also leads to teacher turnover. Without ongoing support or interaction with colleagues, teachers' willingness to stay in the classroom dissolves. In *Beginners in the Classroom* for the Carnegie Foundation on the Advancement of Teaching, Susan Headden (2014) found that the "primary driver of the exodus of early career teachers is a lack of administrative and professional support" (p. 5).

Perhaps the greatest cost of turnover is its impact on achievement of all students in the school. There is a considerable peer effect on other teachers as well. Li Feng and Tim Sass (2011) found that school quality rank plays a significant role in teacher intradistrict mobility. They also found that "peers with job-specific teaching experience, professional certification, and advanced degrees may provide school-specific job skills and knowledge to their colleagues, resulting in lower turnover" (pp. 16–17). Connecting teachers, especially new ones, with their colleagues who can function as mentors and model practice not only strengthens the experience for new teachers, but enriches the quality of instruction for students.

If the traditional schooling culture fails in part to support new classroom teachers, it certainly doesn't serve all students equally. Every parent, teacher, and principal has heard — or voiced — this concern at some point before the start of the school year: "I really hope my child is in Mr. Allen's class next year. How can I make sure that happens?" That is a logical question. Parents and caregivers want their children to have the best possible learning experience in school, and by and large they understand that the quality of teaching is the strongest in-school factor affecting student achievement. As much as principals and teachers may not want to hear that question, raising it is justified because research indicates that there is greater variability of student learning **within** schools than variability of student learning **across** schools (Hattie, 2015). In his paper *What works best in education: The politics of collaborative expertise,* John Hattie (2015) posits that the most important cause of this variability is differences in the effectiveness of teachers; furthermore, he proposes that a logical solution is to build the expertise of all teachers through collaboration (p. 1).

Indeed, education advocates have long championed equitable access to quality education for students regardless of zip code, and that challenge remains in every corner of the country. Still another challenge arises when even in a school recognized as a "good school," all students still aren't experiencing effective teaching. Yet, if the leaders responsible for the learning of every child who attends their schools,

could, as Hattie (2015) suggests, harness and spread the expertise that results in excellent teaching, then all students would find themselves with wonderful learning opportunities.

Teachers realize the value of peer support; in numerous surveys they place high priority on the importance of collaboration with colleagues. For example, in a report on college- and career-ready standards implementation, the National Council on Literacy Education (NCLE) states, "The bottom line is that more time for teacher collaboration leads to more effective standards implementation," (NCLE, 2015, p. 8). Based on educator survey data, the report also suggests a correlation between those schools using specific collaborative learning practices such as co-creating lessons and higher implementation of the standards (NCLE, 2015, p. 8). Research studies continue to indicate that collaboration among teachers contributes to changed practice, in response to specific initiatives, and better results (Kane, Owens, Marinell, Thal, & Staiger, 2016). If all teachers could work in school cultures that support collaborative learning and teaching, they would improve teaching and learning for themselves and all students (see Tool 1.1: Strengthening Your Knowledge About Collaboration for more resources about collaboration and professional learning).

Collaboration is the answer

In Learning Forward's (2011) *Standards for Professional Learning,* educators learning in community is a key structure for addressing many of the problems common in traditional models for improving teaching and learning.

Learning Communities: Professional learning that increases educator effectiveness and results for all students occurs within learning communities committed to continuous improvement, collective responsibility, and goal alignment. (p. 24)

By definition, collaboration reduces isolation for teachers who are learning and improving practice together. Collaborative learning puts teachers in constant structured communication with one another, offering a consistent and reliable means for teachers to find support, solve problems, and grow as a result of working with expert peers. Fortunately, the traditional model of organizing students and educators is shifting somewhat. There are many examples, and some exemplars, of schools and systems that establish collaborative learning cultures and structures to reduce isolation and realize the benefits of teachers' learning and improving with peers (see Tool 1.2: Thinking About Collaborative Learning: Fears and Hopes).

Changing practice

More importantly, learning collaboratively helps teachers change teaching practices. When they have opportunities to meet regularly to discuss authentic classroom challenges, teachers talk specifically about what they do in the classroom and the results they see. With colleagues, they identify problems and solutions. Peer learning structures offer opportunities to pose questions, examine strategies, and experiment in a safe environment with knowledgeable partners.

There is deep expertise within every school, and certainly in the majority of classrooms within every school. Unfortunately, school and system leaders, other teachers, and most sadly, the students, are rarely exposed to all that untapped wisdom. Through well-facilitated collaboration, the expertise and specific practices teachers use successfully come to light. Teachers who are experts in one area or another can demonstrate and discuss exactly what they do, how they do it, when they do it, and how they adapt it in

different situations and contexts. Their teacher learning partners can then ask questions, hone instructional strategies, ask for support, and learn the best ways to integrate such strategies into their own teaching. Emerging research suggests that there is even greater potential of accelerating learning when teachers focus collaborative learning on implementation of high-quality curriculum.

Job satisfaction

Collaboration has an impact on retention and job satisfaction as well as teaching quality. Dion Burns and Linda Darling-Hammond (2014) analyzed data from *Teaching Around the World: What Can TALIS Tell Us?* and found that teacher collaboration was central to teacher effectiveness:

Perhaps the strongest set of findings in TALIS were those associated with teacher collaboration, which appeared as an important element of learning, influence on practice, and influence on job satisfaction and self-efficacy, which are in turn related to teacher retention and effectiveness. More than any other policy area, actions that support collaborative learning among teachers appear to hold promise for improving the quality of teaching.... (p. v)

Similar results were found in the *MetLife Survey of the American Teacher* (2009) where more than two thirds of teachers (67%) and three quarters of principals (78%) say that greater collaboration among teachers and school leaders would have a major impact on improving student achievement. Other findings combine to emphasize that schools with higher degrees of collaboration are associated with shared leadership and higher levels of trust and job satisfaction. Teachers in schools with higher levels of collaborative activities are more likely than others to have high levels of career satisfaction

(68% vs. 54% very satisfied). New teachers strongly agree in greater numbers than do veteran teachers (those with more than 20 years of experience) that their success is linked to that of their colleagues (67% vs. 47%) (MetLife, 2009).

Student outcomes

The most critical benefits of collaboration are in outcomes for students. In the previously mentioned *MetLife Survey* (2009), authors found that teachers who are very satisfied with teaching as a career are more likely than others to have high expectations for their students. In a recent analysis of high-performing systems, Ben Jensen and colleagues (2016) found that collaborative professional learning practices were integrated into the daily work of schools because of their impact on teacher practice and student outcomes. "Teacher professional learning is how they all improve student learning; it is how they improve schools; and it is how they are evaluated in their jobs," they write (Jensen, Sonnemann, Roberts-Hull, & Hunter, 2016, p. 3). The specific practices they found common across four high-performing systems — British Columbia, Hong Kong, Shanghai, and Singapore — engage teachers deeply in collaborative cycles of continuous improvement, very similar to the cycle explored throughout this book.

The beneficiaries of shared expertise are students of teachers who work side by side with other teachers who are experts in their craft. In a two-year period with more than 1,000 teachers, Carrie Leana (2011) found that when 4th- and 5th-grade teachers collaborated purposefully, their instruction improved as did student achievement. Other studies confirm that collaboration among teachers has positive outcomes for students and that working with more skilled peers helps teachers improve (Jackson & Bruegmann, 2009; Sun, Penuel, Frank, Gallagher, & Youngs, 2013).

Structures including schedules, locations, and designs for collaboration also offer teachers opportunities for growth and leadership beyond what they need to learn to instruct the students in their classrooms. Teacher learning teams, for example, require skillful facilitation and leadership, and when teacher leaders are positioned to take on this role, they build their capacity for supporting others and for leading within and beyond the school.

What it takes

The benefits of collaboration don't simply happen when teachers gather in a room. The Gates Foundation (2014) report *Teachers Know Best: Teachers' Views on Professional Development* demonstrates that simply having a team structure in place is insufficient in providing educators with the valuable collective learning they seek. Overall, teachers surveyed were dissatisfied with their professional learning communities and in focus groups they said that collaboration fell short of the ideal. Although they could cite benefits of collaboration, they believed that agendas, protocols, and shared goals are essential (pp. 5–8).

As defined previously on page 5, the Learning Communities standard in Learning Forward's (2011) *Standards for Professional Learning* highlights the essential elements that contribute to improved educational practices and results for all students: "**learning communities committed to continuous improvement, collective responsibility, and goal alignment**" (p. 24). In such communities, learners engage in a cycle of continuous improvement and share responsibility for all students. Their learning is aligned and coherent across teams, schools, and the system (Learning Forward, pp. 24–26).

What, then, do lead learners need to consider to create conditions supportive of collaborative learning?

And what do teachers need to engage in the kinds of collaborative problem solving and intentional learning that they value? Several factors are critical to the implementation of meaningful collaboration: vision and leadership, time, alignment and accountability, clearly defined team goals, facilitation support, collaboration skills, and a commitment to collective responsibility (see Tool 1.3: Reflecting on Meaningful and Effective Professional Learning to consider professional learning experiences).

Vision and leadership

A shared vision for teaching and learning articulates what and how students learn, including both student and educator performance expectations. District and school leaders translate the vision into goals for all learners, whether adults or students. When learners share a deep understanding of the vision and goals, they become clear about their role in helping to achieve both. When teachers and members of learning teams participate in establishing, clarifying, and communicating the vision for all learners, they can become lead learners themselves and have confidence about their role in building and sustaining a learning culture (see Tool 1.4: Assessing the Current State and Determining Next Actions to begin planning a course of action for collaborative professional learning).

Principals and district administrators also support collaborative learning when they ensure that all educators have the resources they require, including research-based resources, high-quality curriculum and instructional materials, and time. Resources, however, are only part of a supportive environment. Learning teams benefit when school and system leaders engage as learners on the teams. Leader participation supports coherence and alignment across a school and a system. Also, when principals participate as learners on teams, they become more skillful instructional leaders, and,

most importantly, demonstrate the importance of continuous learning for all, a critical factor in creating learning cultures in schools. School leaders who value continuous learning not only will talk about it as a way of working, but will also tend the process of continuous learning. They realize that learning teams may develop solutions or effect change gradually. But supportive leaders also recognize the effort and evidence that may support a team's long-term understanding and commitment to applying continuous improvement for themselves and students.

Time

When educators talk about their learning needs, they cite time as a key resource they need to engage in collaborative learning. Without schedules that guarantee time embedded throughout the workweek, educators have no hope of participating in ongoing purposeful collaborative learning. In addition to ensuring and protecting time, figuring out how much time is enough time becomes another challenge. School leaders tackling those challenges can engage teacher teams in helping to figure out "what" and "how" questions related to time. After all, for teacher teams to realize the benefit of collaboration, they need opportunities to meet regularly, consistently, during the work week (Killion, 2013). School leaders, other staff, and the teams themselves must protect learning-team time and not use it to address other priorities. If teachers intend to implement the learning and improvement cycle covered throughout this book, they need to know that they will have dedicated blocks of time to start, continue, and sustain the work for the duration of the school year.

Many school systems are responding to this need for time by creating schedules that allow teams to meet regularly within the designated workday rather than only before or after school. Unfortunately, many of those systems do so without communicating a clear plan for using the time effectively or providing the other resources and support that make meaningful collaboration possible. There is a danger in providing time without other supports. If both educators and community members see that professional learning time is wasted, they are not likely to support changed schedules for long, given that implementing such schedules can be difficult for a school system. Time is a necessary resource, yet not sufficient (Killion, 2013) for ensuring that teachers learn collaboratively. Leaders who want to get the most from their investment in collaborative learning have a clear vision and rationale for using it.

Alignment and accountability

As discussed previously (see page 7, "What it takes"), Learning Forward's Learning Communities standard cites the importance of alignment among school and system goals along with policies and structures to support learning communities. Such alignment prevents fragmentation among learning communities. School and system leaders intentionally align learning communities within and across schools "with an explicit vision and goals for successful learning communities. Learning communities align their goals with those of the school and school system, engage in continuous professional learning, and hold all members collectively accountable for results" (Learning Forward, 2011, p. 26).

Bolstered with such alignment, teacher learning teams may undertake their work each day and each week with an understanding of how their learning goals fit into school- and systemwide plans. They also understand that they are accountable for not only maintaining such alignment but ensuring that their work as a team contributes to the goals and real results for students.

Clear team goals and learning protocols

When educators understand specifically why they are meeting, they are more likely to benefit from collaboration. In a cycle of continuous improvement, as the following chapters will cover, teams examine many sources of data to pinpoint student learning needs and achievement gaps and go from there to determine their own learning needs. They will develop a plan for monitoring progress toward achievement of their goals and communicating the results (see "Chapter 7: Monitor, Assess, and Adjust Practice.") With a guiding vision in place and system- and schoolwide commitment to alignment and coherence, each team is ready to establish and strive toward the achievement of specific goals for themselves and their students.

Facilitation support

Although most teachers are eager to collaborate, they don't necessarily step into their first team meeting prepared to use the time effectively. Here's where skillful facilitation is essential. Educators in many roles can be capable facilitators — teachers, principals, department heads, instructional coaches — anyone who has had the opportunity develop the knowledge and skills to facilitate teams of adult learners. Facilitators help to structure time use, develop team norms and agendas, and select protocols for a wide range of purposes. And as noted above, developing such skills is a wonderful growth opportunity for teachers.

Collaboration skills

While skilled facilitators assist high-functioning teams in meeting their goals and using time wisely, each teacher on a learning team also needs opportunities to understand, practice, and apply a range of collaboration skills. They may intentionally build such understanding within or beyond their team learning time, wherever they have opportunities to learn foundational skills and practices in communication, decision making, and conflict resolution, to name a few. As all team learners become more experienced, they develop deeper skills in collaboration and are able to share more equally in team leadership.

Commitment to collective responsibility

When all teachers on a team take responsibility for every learner in the school, whether student or adult, collective responsibility is the outcome. Learning Forward believes that collective responsibility creates truly equitable learning environments. If teachers know they hold the future of every student in their hands, they take actions that support their peers, whether through sharing expertise, co-teaching, offering a sounding board, or intervening when students are in danger. In such learning cultures, all students truly do have access to the best teaching a school has to offer. Reality dictates that the teacher who might be labeled the expert on any given strategy or topic can't be in every classroom when she is needed. Collaborative learning structures, therefore, provide the best forum for spreading that expertise to other teachers through discussion, practice, observation, and assessment.

When conditions are less than ideal

How can teachers and teacher teams learn productively when they don't have the ideal support, resources, or culture for learning? As this chapter has described, not every school or system possesses the conditions that are best for team learning. Moreover, within in any system, even those that more generally support collaborative learning, individual educators experience different levels of understanding about the value of collaborative learning. Certainly, the expectation would be that educators across the system would advocate for the resources and conditions educators require for optimal learning. Given that professionals embrace new ways of working at different rates of speed, these suggestions serve the trend-setting teachers who are ready to learn and breaking collaborative ground, if need be:

Identify and connect with allies

As a professional each teacher who participates in a learning team likely already has a network of sorts within his or her building or system. Every member, at least, has an idea about who shares some of his or her concerns or challenges and who might have expertise to offer. Members reach out informally to the teachers who they believe could be valuable learning peers. In finding out more about these colleagues, proactive team members may begin to talk about how they might help one another.

Don't start from scratch

Perhaps a simple collaboration could build on something that's already happening. For example, if a middle school math team went to a district-sponsored professional learning session in the summer, consider a small-scale follow up. Team members may reach out to a couple of colleagues and ask them what they've done with a particular lesson or topic. A manageable beginning is to create the opportunity to talk for 15 minutes about it before school one day. Whatever learning opportunity the team is able to create — meet regularly, observe one another, review student work — members need to find ways to collect evidence and record their progress.

Start small

Fledgling teams may identify a collaborative learning task that seems relatively easy to accomplish.

That is, they define a goal that they could achieve without too much additional time or money. For example, they could share a short article about an intriguing strategy they haven't tried and see if they could carve out 10 minutes at the next department meeting to find out whether others have. In doing so, they model the kinds of interactions they'd like to experience on a bigger scale by engaging in a substantive discussion about the challenges and benefits of a particular strategy.

Define a specific challenge

Everyone recognizes that collaboration for collaboration's sake isn't meaningful. Intentional teams will keep a collective eye on the big picture and often remind one another, "What is it we're hoping to address?" Teams that have identified a colleague or two who share similar students or challenges, may be able to define a very specific problem for which they want to develop solutions. Individual members may set goals for themselves, if not for the full team, that define what each wants to accomplish so he or she can keep that time productive and focused.

Join a virtual community of learners

Team members who can't seem to find willing colleagues nearby, may look to the Internet to find individuals with whom to collaborate. A benefit of many states adopting similar college- and career-ready standards is that teachers across the country can find other teachers who share expectations for students; they can begin to share expertise, tools, and resources while they work on common problems.

Propose a pilot team

If a school or system has similar expectations, and teachers find a willing band of colleagues who want to work together on a specific challenge, they would approach the principal or other school leader and explain that the team wants to embark on an action research project. Exercising their agency to show that they are knowledgeable and committed, the team members could also demonstrate that they believe they are ready to undertake lesson study. Although their particular culture may not offer resources or other support, the group of teachers could at least request recognition that their team is at work. Then, team members could also take on the responsibility to share, even informally, what they achieved and what they learned.

Become the expert on collaboration. How can professionals who aspire to work in a collaborative culture, help others understand the value of such a working environment? They may gather evidence of how collaboration helps educators improve and learn about the strategies that make collaboration effective. They connect with colleagues in other systems virtually, if need be, to build their own success stories.

Celebrate and document results. Whatever form the initial collaborative learning takes, teams need to share information about the outcomes and help others understand what those outcomes mean. Teams will find it beneficial to follow up on even the smallest collaborations because those communications help colleagues and supervisors see what collegial interactions did to bolster team members' attitudes, knowledge, and skills. For example, if a team managed to address a defined goal with other colleagues in its school, team members might ask for the opportunity to present their process and outcomes at a meeting. With regular, even informal, communications a team not only shares their knowledge and developing expertise, they also give school leaders a rationale and evidence for committing more time and resources to similar work.

Reflections

• We can articulate the benefits of collaborative learning.
• We can advocate for the value of collaborative professional learning.
• We know what elements are critical to supporting meaningful collaboration in schools.
• We have actions to take to help create collaborative cultures and learning structures.
• We have resources to consult to learn more about collaborative learning.

Keep the end in mind

The ultimate goal of collaborative learning is better teaching, better student learning, better results for every learner in schools. Collaboration done intentionally, deeply, and daily creates new cultures in schools that lead to professionalism in teaching, job satisfaction, stability in staff and teaching quality. As Jensen and colleagues (2016) found in *Beyond PD,* "[h]igh-performing systems transform the improvement cycle into a culture of continuous professional learning that, in time, turns schools into true learning organizations" (p. 5).

Excellent teams — supported by committed leaders and sustained resources — create a culture in which every professional in a school takes responsibility for every student. Who wouldn't want to work in a such a culture? More importantly, who wouldn't want his or her child to learn in such an environment, supported by a building full of continual learners committed to figuring out what every student needs most and finding ways to make it happen?

References

Bill & Melinda Gates Foundation. (2014, December). *Teachers know best: Teachers' views on professional development.* Seattle, WA: Author. Available at http://k12education.gatesfoundation.org/wp-content/uploads/2015/04/Gates-PDMarket Research-Dec5.pdf

Burns, D. & Darling-Hammond, L. (2014, December). *Teaching around the world: What can TALIS tell us.* Available at https://edpolicy.stanford.edu/publications/pubs/1295

Feng, L. & Sass, T. (2012, February). *Teacher quality and teacher mobility.* Washington, DC: National Center for the Analysis of Longitudinal Data in Education Research (CALDER).

Hattie, J. (2015, June). *What works best in education: The politics of collaborative expertise.* Available at https://www.pearson.com/content/dam/corporate/global/pearson-dot-com/files/hattie/150526_ExpertiseWEB_V1.pdf

Headden, S. (2014). *Beginners in the classroom: What the changing demographics of teaching mean for schools, students, and society.* Stanford, CA: Carnegie Foundation for the Advancement of Teaching.

Jackson, C. K. & Bruegmann, E. (2009.) Teaching students and teaching each other: The importance of peer learning for teachers. *American Economic Journal: Applied Economics 1*(4), 1–33.

Jensen, B., Sonnemann, J., Roberts-Hull, K., & Hunter, A. (2016). *Beyond PD: Teacher professional learning in high-performing systems.* Available at www.ncee.org/wp-content/uploads/2016/02/Beyond PDWebv2.pdf

Kane, T. J., Owens, M., Marinell, W.H., Thal, D.R.C., & Staiger, D.O. (2016). *Teaching higher: Educators' perspectives on common core implementation.* Cambridge, MA: Center for Education Policy Research, Harvard University.

Killion, J. (2013). *Establishing time for professional learning.* Oxford, OH: Learning Forward. Available to members at https://learningforward.org/docs/default-source/commoncore/establishing-time-for-professional-learning.pdf?sfvrsn=6

Leana, C. (2011, Fall). The missing link in school reform. *Stanford Social Innovation Review,* 30–35.

Learning Forward. (2011). *Standards for Professional Learning.* Oxford, OH: Author.

MetLife, Inc. (2010, April). *The 2009 MetLife survey of the American teacher: Collaborating for student success.* Available at https://eric.ed.gov/?id=ED509650

Meyer, J. (2009, April). Researcher: Teacher improvement plateaus after 4 years. In Colorado Classroom. [Weblog]. *The Denver Post.* Available at http://blogs.denverpost.com/colorado classroom/2009/04/

NCLE (National Center for Literacy Education). (2015). *Building literacy capacity: The conditions for effective standards implementation.* Available at www.literacyinlearningexchange.org/sites/default/files/2015nclesurveyreport_framing.pdf

Sun, M., Penuel, W.R., Frank, K.A., Gallagher, H.R., & Youngs, P. (2013). Shaping professional development to promote the diffusion of instructional expertise among teachers. *Educational Evaluation and Policy Analysis, 35*(3), 344–369.

Tools index for chapter 1

Tool	Title	Use
1.1	Strengthening your knowledge about collaboration	Use this tool to become familiar with some of the research examining collaboration among teachers as one feature of effective professional learning.
1.2	Thinking about collaborative learning: Fears and hopes	Use this tool to identify the fears, concerns, and hopes associated with collaborative learning.
1.3	Reflecting on meaningful and effective professional learning	Use this tool to reflect on and compare previous learning experiences with the big ideas that characterize effective collaborative professional learning.
1.4	Assessing the current state and determining next actions	Use this set of tools to conduct a SWOT (strengths, weaknesses, opportunities, and threats) analysis to develop an action plan to implement a team decision.

CHAPTER 2

The learning team cycle promotes continuous improvement

Where are we now?

We are committed to implementing a learning team cycle.

STRONGLY AGREE   AGREE   NO OPINION   DISAGREE   STRONGLY DISAGREE

We determine or refine student learning goals in alignment with a vision of good teaching and learning at the district or school level.

STRONGLY AGREE   AGREE   NO OPINION   DISAGREE   STRONGLY DISAGREE

Our own learning is grounded in the challenges our students face.

STRONGLY AGREE   AGREE   NO OPINION   DISAGREE   STRONGLY DISAGREE

We have access to multiple sources of data that we use to inform our learning.

STRONGLY AGREE   AGREE   NO OPINION   DISAGREE   STRONGLY DISAGREE

We monitor and reflect on our learning goals to know whether we're making progress.

STRONGLY AGREE   AGREE   NO OPINION   DISAGREE   STRONGLY DISAGREE

We can schedule our learning in alignment with key student goals and dates.

STRONGLY AGREE   AGREE   NO OPINION   DISAGREE   STRONGLY DISAGREE

Overview

Educators and quality-management practitioners in other professions often speak of improvement, learning, or change as happening in a cycle. In its most basic form such a cycle occurs when active learners — whether adults or children — observe the world around them, take action based on what they understand, and then reflect on what happened before they plan their next steps, usually modifying their actions to better achieve the results they seek.

This chapter reviews application of cycles of continuous improvement in education organizations, covers the five stages of Learning Forward's learning team cycle, and offers reflection questions and tools for further work (see Tool 2.1: Understanding the Five Stages for more information about the learning team cycle).

How does a team set a context for learning and continuous improvement?

Teachers may bring their individual learning to bear on activities in classrooms and schools, but the more they can apply and refine that learning within a collective activity, the more quickly the culture of continuous improvement grows. When teachers seize opportunities to create, lead, and learn in teams, they and their students benefit — if the teams understand how to frame the purpose and focus of their work.

After all, a mandate to collaborate may begin a team's work together, but it will not help them achieve success. Michael Fullan has drawn attention to the fact that collaboration too often is structured without the intentionality required to get positive, measurable student results (Hirsh, 2016). The learning cycle creates

such a structure: It promotes "collaboration and collective responsibility within a teacher team by setting up structures for short-term cycles of improvement" (Michigan Department of Education, n.d.). *Plan, do, reflect* is a commonly used three-step cycle, and a well-known four-stage cycle, also known as the Deming Cycle, is the *plan, do, check, act* cycle (American Society for Quality, n.d., para. 3). Bruce Wellman and Laura Lipton (2009) advance their Collaborative Learning Cycle of *activating and engaging, exploring and discovering, and organizing and integrating* (p. 5).

Learning Forward's Standards for Professional Learning put a cycle of continuous improvement at the heart of collaborative learning. The standards embody a belief that a *learning team cycle* is the day-to-day means for embedding professional learning in classrooms, thus supporting teachers when they need it most. There are many forms of learning cycles, cycles of inquiry, or cycles of continuous improvement. Within professional learning in education alone, educators can find several examples.

In their professional learning community work, the DuFours and Robert Eaker (2008) have said that a learning team collaborates to determine (a) What is it that they want students to know? (b) How will they know if students know it? and (c) What will they do if students do know or don't know it? To learn the answers to those questions, DuFour and colleagues (2010) note that learning communities use a cycle of inquiry that includes five stages: gathering evidence of student learning, developing strategies to address weaknesses and strengths in that learning, implementing new strategies, analyzing the impact of new strategies, and applying new knowledge in the next cycle of continuous improvement (DuFour, DuFour, Eaker, & Many, 2010).

Inquiry cycles are central to both lesson study and action research learning designs, for example. In lesson study, teams of teachers focus intently on specific classroom lessons. They consider carefully which short- and long-term student learning goals to emphasize, collaboratively plan a lesson, teach the lesson while colleagues observe, and then discuss and revise the lesson based on what they learn about the results of the lesson and its effect on student learning; often, other team members teach the next iteration (Lewis, 2014). In action research, Richard Sagor (2000) outlines a seven-step process that begins with selecting a focus and continues through clarifying theories, identifying research questions, collecting data, analyzing data, reporting results, and taking action informed by what teachers learn from data analysis.

The National School Reform Faculty (2014) also promotes a cycle of inquiry for professional learning, developed by the Southern Maine Partnership. The stages are analyzing data, framing or reframing key issues, investigating literature and expertise, developing an action plan, and carrying out strategies and collecting data.

Finally, in Anne Jolly's (2008) *Team to Teach: A Facilitator's Guide for Professional Learning,* learning teams use a collaborative decision-making cycle with the following steps: identify student needs, examine studies and research, engage in rigorous reflection, use research and wisdom to make good choices, collaboratively experiment with new teaching practices, monitor and assess implementation, communicate information to other stakeholders (p. 29).

These examples are not exhaustive, but they demonstrate the field's widespread support for an iterative process that deeply engages educators in the work of studying student needs, preparing lessons, assessing their own knowledge, and reflecting on specific practices to inform next steps. Such cycles offer meaningful opportunities for teachers to put student understanding front and center, inquire collaboratively into what they as educators know and don't know how to do, and discuss their impact on student learning. Teachers using a learning team cycle begin with a plan that anticipates how their learning and instructional choices will affect what students know and are able to do. They will adjust those plans as they build skills, knowledge, and dispositions while they move through the cycle.

What is the learning team cycle?

In this book, the learning team cycle is a five-stage process aligned with Learning Forward's Standards for Professional Learning to guide the learning team's work (see Figure 2.1). The descriptions on pages 19–22 briefly describe each stage of the learning team cycle; Chapters 3 through 7 examine the stages and procedures to implement them in more detail.

Entering the cycle

Once they decide to use a learning cycle, how do school-based learning teams know which student learning gap they're going to address during their time together? In a coherent and aligned system, this work will be driven by the system's common vision for good instruction. Communicated through content standards, instructional frameworks, and performance standards, the vision for a system makes clear to every educator what students will know and be able to do; thus, an articulated vision drives teachers' performance expectations. In their effort to identify a focus area, which is aligned with district and school goals, the team may also review strategic priorities; systemwide, school and individual goals for improvement; and school improvement plans (see more discussion in Chapter 9).

When teachers move from the district's common vision to the collaborative work they're going to

Figure 2.1: Teacher learning team cycle

Analyze data

Examine student and educator learning challenges:
- Identify and collect essential data
- Organize and display data for analysis
- Examine data for trends, issues, and opportunities
- Summarize the data

Monitor, assess, and adjust practice

Use evidence to assess and refine implementation and impact:
- Collect formative and summative data
- Monitor progress toward goals
- Analyze data and reflect on outcomes
- Refine and determine next actions

Set goals

Identify shared goals for student and educator learning:
- Review summary statements and set priorities
- Write student goals
- Write teacher goals
- Review with others

Implement new learning

Implement refined lessons and assessments with local support in the classroom:
- Develop plan for implementing units and lessons
- Use tools or resources to guide implementation and support adaptation as necessary
- Enlist job-embedded support
- Engage in feedback process with evidence from others to inform continuous improvement

Learn individually and collaboratively

Gain new knowledge and skills; examine assumptions, aspirations, and beliefs:
- Set learning priorities
- Write team and individual learning agendas
- Practice new learning
- Schedule and engage in learning

address as a team, they identify their area of focus broadly in several ways. They are likely to funnel down from a general goal tied to the common vision to the specifics addressed by their grade-level or subject-matter teams. In doing so, they examine relevant data, including different types of student assessments, accountability measures, and maybe examples of student work. Examples of considerations that might drive a team's challenge include the following:

- The district has identified a systemwide improvement priority for all teams: *We're focusing on academic language skills for all students with a particular emphasis on English Language Learners.*

- The school has identified particular improvement goals based on the previous years' assessments: *Our school will raise our proficiency in ELA by 15%, mathematics by 8%, and science by 8%.*

- The grade levels in a school have identified specific content standards that need attention: *We will improve our third graders' understanding and use of fractions this year.*

- The subject-matter teams have identified specific content standards that need attention: *The social studies teachers will focus on improving students' text comprehension and discussion skills.*

Because teachers regularly tackle numerous challenges, they will be addressing several student learning improvement goals at the same time. Teachers, first, need to prioritize which learning challenge they can best address with learning teams. Then, they can apply the five-stage learning team cycle and determine, together, the appropriate problem to resolve. A team may find that the problem jumps out at them after they analyze the most recent assessment data. Or they may realize the root problem after they examine data showing performance differences among subgroups of students within a grade level. Members make their own decisions about how they choose a problem and make it a priority to study and address. To take advantage of such flexibility, team members will want to be familiar with the entire cycle.

Moving through each stage

Each chapter of this book will examine in depth one of the five stages described here.

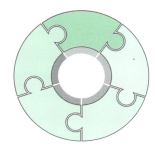

Analyze data: Examine student and educator learning challenges

In this stage, team members analyze data so they can identify and better understand the exact problem they are addressing. For example, although a team's schoolwide goal might be to increase reading comprehension, only by looking at student data will members know exactly which elements of reading comprehension are problematic or which areas of the curriculum raise concerns; who is struggling and who is succeeding. Depending on their sources of data, educators may also get information identifying teachers who have been more successful and might be good sources of information about instructional strategies.

To use data successfully teams need to work in a culture where they embrace the use of data. School leaders will consider how to create a supportive culture in which teachers benefit from professional learning and other supports to develop knowledge and skills to use data effectively and avoid becoming overwhelmed by the quantity of data. Team members will access, examine, and interpret data to write data summary statements.

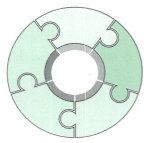

Set goals: Identify shared goals for student and educator learning

At this stage teams discuss their data summary statements and select student and team learning goals. These goals align with the school system and school improvement goals yet are specific to the needs of their students and the units or lessons coming up in the curriculum. At that point, they can set specific student learning goals, expressed as SMART goals: specific, measurable, attainable, results-based, and timebound.

During this stage the team is writing an actionable learning plan that includes the development of classroom strategies and the timing for learning about and using those strategies (throughout the five-stage cycle, teams may use Tool 2.2: Reviewing the Learning Team Cycle to begin and track progress on their cycles). After the team determines what their students need to know and be able to do, they turn their attention to what the adults must learn and be able to do to help achieve student goals. For example, from their data they see that lower-performing students consistently lag behind in grade-level vocabulary development. The team members may realize that as teachers, they need to learn different instructional and classroom strategies tied to rigorous vocabulary use. Depending on the student learning goal(s) they've set, teachers may find that they need to focus on any of a range of improvement goals for themselves, from developing content knowledge, to trying new instructional strategies, to using technology to engage with particular groups of students in different ways.

Team members take a critical step by setting their own learning goals. If they don't set learning goals for themselves, they may resort to applying what they already know, which is presumably what produced the previous results. Or they may find themselves experimenting with new strategies without a deep understanding or sufficient preparation to implement those new strategies with fidelity.

Yet, setting goals may challenge teams, sometimes, because individuals may find it difficult to identify what they think they know and what they need to know. Teams may mitigate the challenge with individual or collective self-assessment. A powerful mechanism for professional growth, self-assessment contributes to a teacher's belief about his or her self-efficacy. Researchers John Ross and Cathy Bruce (2007) find that teacher efficacy influences goal setting. So, teachers who have strong self-efficacy are likely to set high goals for themselves and their students.

This stage paves the way for ensuring that educator learning is intentional and tied directly to what students need to learn. Without explicit outcomes stated for both educators and students, team members may lack clarity about their beliefs and understanding of how their practices influence what students take away from the classroom. During this stage of the cycle, team members articulate the links between their practices and student understanding. They are also deliberate in addressing not only the knowledge and skills they need to meet student learning needs but also the behaviors, attitudes, and aspirations essential to continuous improvement.

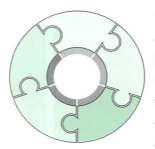

Learn individually and collaboratively: Gain new knowledge and skills (e.g. content and content-specific pedagogy); examine assumptions, aspirations, and beliefs

When teams know their own improvement goals, they are ready to engage in learning to change their attitudes, build their knowledge and skills, and improve their practices. Constantly focusing on the learning goals they set for themselves and their students will help them choose appropriate learning experiences. The curriculum and instructional materials they use with students will guide their learning. Team members will study the student and educator materials carefully to determine the specific content of their learning and to identify additional gaps in their own expertise.

Team members also need to decide how they might best differentiate their individual learning, especially when they begin to learn as a team. They may seek deliberate facilitation from a colleague or coach so that each team member can say what he or she would like to learn to address the learning goal. If teams believe that they lack knowledge of learning designs, they may seek guidance from a colleague, district staff member, principal, or consultant who can advise them on design options.

While the team may have set collective goals to achieve, each team member has his or her own learning preferences, works at a particular career stage, and already has a unique level of content and pedagogical expertise tied to the goal. At first, teams may need to be explicit about how they address and accommodate their differences; they may want to assign roles in meetings (see Tool 2.3: Creating Purposeful Team Roles) to help inventory and clarify roles that contribute to the team function. As they learn together during the course of a cycle, members will better understand how each learns as well as what each brings to the work. Over time their learning and working together will likely become more fluid.

Once they have clarity about the specific learning needs and inclinations of each team member, team members can identify expertise and learning design options. They may seek information resources for book study. With the student curriculum as the basis for what happens in the classroom each day, teachers explore their instructional materials to review upcoming units and identify where they need to develop deeper content or pedagogical expertise. Then they determine how to approach their learning to achieve their goals. If they lack expertise in the building or district, teams may look elsewhere, perhaps an online network, course, webinar, or a technical assistance provider with a specialty focus. They may seek coaching on using particular strategies from their principal, an instructional coach in their building or district, or a coach on the team.

Learning may take many forms at this stage, and team members engage as active participants throughout the process; as part of their learning, they are looking ahead to application. Perhaps they take advantage of practice sessions or consult with peers who have successfully used the chosen strategies in the past. Whatever their choices, team members incorporate what they are learning into their lesson planning and student assessments as they ready themselves to use new tools, content, and ideas.

Implement new learning: Implement refined lessons and assessments with local support in the classroom

At this stage, team members take their learning into their classrooms. Although they may have had opportunities to try out strategies with peers, teachers only apply their learning in the classroom when they change their practices and behaviors in ways that affect what and how students learn.

Teachers' knowledge and skills will multiply as they apply their new learning in different contexts. As they become more familiar with new strategies, they become more skilled both in implementing new learning with fidelity and getting useful support from coaches and peers to improve. The first steps in the implementation of new knowledge rarely lead immediately to the intended outcome. Even at the classroom level, teachers can experience the *implementation dip,* or the point at which new practices at first show a decline in results. Change, after all, takes time, and moving a group of learners forward is a long-range process.

With positive supporting conditions, teachers may receive guidance from coaches or peers to apply their learning throughout this stage. Perhaps they co-teach a lesson with a peer; a coach may observe and support the teacher before, during, and after implementation by posing questions and offering suggestions. Or, team members may use video as a tool throughout the learning and application of new knowledge.

Monitor, assess, and adjust practice: Use evidence to assess and refine implementation and impact

After teachers take new practices into classrooms, they begin to watch how their new knowledge and instructional strategies affect what happens in the classroom. They gather evidence, which may take many forms, of the implementation of their learning. Not only do they watch how students respond during class time, they also collect data and information from classroom assessments and student work. For each student learning goal that they set, teams develop formative and summative assessments that measure precisely what they hoped to achieve.

Teams examine this evidence and consider whether new classroom practices are helping them achieve their goals. They also measure their use of instructional strategies. With this information, team members may realize they are on the right track and can refine the ways they are teaching students. They may also realize that their changes in practice aren't contributing to student learning, in which case they will adjust their assumptions and review their skills and practices. They'll need to consider several questions as they review and adjust: Did they make the right assumptions when they set their own learning goals? Did they engage in appropriate learning that really helped them achieve their learning goals? Did they learn what they needed before they put the strategy into practice? Did they implement the new learning with fidelity and get sufficient support in applying their learning in the classroom?

When teams have answered these questions, they are ready to advance to the next stage of the learning team cycle (or go back if they need to revisit a previous stage) so they may continue making progress toward better student outcomes.

How do teams apply the learning team cycle?

A big question for learning teams is, "How will we schedule their meeting time specifically to work through the stages?" This book proposes a 12-week cycle that takes teams through the five stages. In any specific school setting, of course, a team may need to adjust the schedule based on the time they have allocated for team meetings, the timing of assessment reports, the curriculum and instructional materials they use, the particular learning design(s) they choose, and myriad other factors that contribute to the pacing of both adult and student learning.

The example 12-week schedule (see Figure 2.2) is based on several critical assumptions:

- Teachers have three or more hours per week to dedicate to learning collaboratively with their teams.
- Teachers have access to the data they need to understand student learning gaps and set meaningful goals.
- Teachers are motivated to change short- and long-term lessons based on what they learn together.
- Teachers can set their learning schedules so that the application stage has them teaching an improved or augmented lesson during Week Seven of the cycle.
- Teachers work both individually and collectively on the problems they identify together: The learning doesn't happen solely during team time.
- Teachers have ready access to learning support within the school or district.
- Teachers work in a culture that prioritizes continuous learning for adults with a climate where trust pervades all interactions.
- Teachers know generally where their greatest student learning gaps lie, informed by school and system improvement goals.
- Teachers have the expertise and support to collaborate efficiently during limited collaboration time.

As teams become more experienced in using this cycle, and as schools develop a more inquiry-oriented culture, two things may happen to advance this work:

1. Team members and principals will develop a better sense of how to schedule multiple overlapping cycles in ways that support the entire instructional calendar; and
2. Team members will naturally think in more reflective ways at each stage of the process, and while

they are working through a particular stage, will be incorporating elements of other stages at the same time. That is, though they may be setting goals in Stage 2, they're already doing a certain amount of learning. Or while they are learning collaboratively in Stage 3, they're already actively reflecting on how they will apply those learnings in Stage 4 and carefully considering the intended impact on practice in Stage 5.

Figure 2.2 outlines the stages through 18 weeks to show how two learning cycles overlap. During a learning cycle, members of a team are unlikely to study all of their lessons together, but they do improve lessons with units that address high-priority learning goals. In this example, the team is learning to use visual models, including fraction bars, number lines, and area models to produce quotients of whole numbers and fractions. For each of two units, they are improving five week-long lessons, identifying common student errors, and developing responses to assist students in correcting those errors.

The team invests six weeks in data analysis, goal setting, intentional learning, and lesson improvement and assessment development before introducing Unit A. Soon after they begin teaching the unit, team members gather information from formative assessments and other monitoring tools to inform any changes they decide to make to their plan.

Things will rarely go as planned; however, having a desired vision gives the team a structure to support its work. And while the team is implementing its plan for Unit A, it will begin the process of planning for Unit B. The calendar shows the complexity of the work and why each stage is so important. Throughout the five-stage cycle, teams may refer to Tool 2.4: Scheduling a Learning Team Cycle to consider the stages, indicators, and a schedule for their learning cycles.

Figure 2.2: Scheduling two learning cycles

Week	1	2	3	4	5	6	7	8	9	10	11	12	13	14	15	16	17	18
Stage 1: Analyze data	Learning Cycle 1						Learning Cycle 2											
Stage 2: Set goals		Learning Cycle 1						Learning Cycle 2										
Stage 3: Learn individually and collaboratively			Learning Cycle 1							Learning Cycle 2								
Stage 4: Implement new learning							Learning Cycle 1						Learning Cycle 2					
Stage 5: Monitor, assess, and adjust practice										Learning Cycle 1					Learning Cycle 2			

Plan for time

Years ago, a large urban district lobbied diligently for learning time for teachers. The district leaders heard the demand, loud and clear, from teachers: "We need time to meet with each other!" So the leaders enacted a plan that gave teachers two hours of learning time a week. Within eight weeks, the schedule reverted to its previous timing.

When Learning Forward visited with union leaders to understand what happened, they shared that no one had an idea about what they were supposed to do with the additional two hours a week. "What's the plan?" parents had wanted to know.

In fact, there was no plan, and that valuable opportunity — and much good will — was wasted.

— Stephanie Hirsh

Factors that influence cycle timing

Earlier in Chapter 2 the discussion of a continuous improvement cycle pointed out that the flexibility of the cycle supports teams in their own learning. Applying a cycle means team members pay attention to individual meetings and to what they need to do during each meeting to ensure completion of all stages. At the same time, teams also need to focus on the collective success of the cycle across longer time frames. Teams may enter the cycle at any point based on analysis of data or other feedback and their learning needs. Throughout this process, team members receive feedback (in the form of data from assessments or information from observations or study of student work) that shows them whether (and how) each of their choices leads to the outcome they anticipate. What they learn will help team members make assessments and adjustments that lead them forward in the learning cycle. How teams use the cycle or how much time they spend at each stage, depends on the following factors: scope of the goal, level of development of the group, and knowledge and expertise of the group.

Scope of the goal

The team may not be able to focus as tightly on a student learning objective as this timing presumes. They may be driven by school or system standards, curriculum, goals, and objectives to address an even broader systemwide goal. Their educator effectiveness process may prioritize goals at still another scale.

Development of the group

If a learning team is just forming, its members may not yet fully trust one another in ways that lead to efficient collaboration. If a learning team doesn't contain members skilled in facilitation in collaboration, it may need to spend time getting up to speed in that arena to sustain long-term improvement.

Knowledge and expertise of the group

The members of the team may be at different career stages or levels of classroom experience and need more time for learning. Having a team with members of varying levels of skill and experience can benefit a learning team, particularly if the more experienced members are willing to contribute what they know, yet without taking over the decision making of the team.

The team may not contain much internal expertise or may need to tap external sources more often. So, how does a learning team know when it needs to draw on outside expertise at any stage of a learning cycle? The answer may be simple: Every team member may know from experience and data that he or she knows little or nothing about how to begin to address the challenge the team faces. But even when team members know they need to seek outside expertise, they consider a range of questions as they set goals and plan their learning:

- Do we know of others in the building who have success with this or other student learning challenges?
- What have we experienced as learners that helps us consider where to turn?
- How can our coach or principal guide us toward information and people to determine next steps?

Answering these questions will help team members decide whether and how to turn beyond the team to advance their progress toward the learning goals. We discuss this more in "Chapter 5: Learn individually and collaboratively."

Putting learning teams to work

Many school and system leaders understand that learning teams or professional learning communities (PLCs) are valuable structures for ensuring that educators have time to learn in collaboration with colleagues. Some district leaders establish team time with a clear vision for exactly what the learning teams will do, including how they will use their time together and what results they are expected to achieve. Read the vignette on page 26 to see how a district superintendent in Ontario has grown to value and support collaborative, job-embedded team learning.

Other district leaders have been convinced that PLCs would be great, so they create schedules that allow teams to meet, but they lack a plan or vision for what those teams will do during that time. They trust that the professionals will know what to do with the time. Setting aside team time without a plan is a professional hazard. Districts go to a lot of trouble to rearrange schedules, engage with parents, and expend considerable energy with teachers and unions. If that time isn't well spent, everyone involved will label team learning a waste, and professional learning

Letting a bright light burn — Leaders create conditions for learning

As I enter the third decade of my career, I reflect on what I believe are the conditions that contribute to educators' continuous professional development of the art and science of teaching and learning: contextual information and space, collaboration, and leadership. Early in my teaching career, I found that having accurate information about my students and being able to learn in my working environment kept my learning relevant. I also connected more deeply to my day-to-day practice. Trusting and learning-focused professional relationships with colleagues gave me the right amount of tension and support to let me take risks and deepen my learning and understanding. I also thought it was abundantly clear that leadership had the power to make or break a learning culture. It hardly matters how bright the light of a classroom teacher is; if leaders do not recognize and create the conditions to support continuous professional learning, they will extinguish that light.

In my role as superintendent, a pivotal point for me as a leader came when we created school-based learning time. I took the opportunity, with the leadership team, to listen to school faculties, educators, and formal leaders. In focus group interviews staff from a variety of positions throughout the organization stated clearly what they wanted time to collaborate, reflect, and examine their practice. Educators wanted to witness learning in action, not in a ballroom. They wanted to be closest to student learning, and they wanted to learn together. As a senior team, we became a responsive organization when we provided exactly what they said they needed. First, we directed a predominant amount of central office professional development dollars proportionally to schools to determine the when, the how, and the why of professional learning time. We referred to this as school-based learning time. Then, with the allocation of that time, we attached some non-negotiables, one of which was that there would be a direct connection to the Board Improvement Plan for Achievement and the district strategic plan. As school-based learning time has become a regular practice in our system, we have analyzed qualitative and quantitative data to track its effectiveness. Literacy scores continue to improve in our elementary schools and our staff are better able to connect to the Board Improvement Plan as well as articulate what they do and why they do it.

For a district to be a learning organization, learning must occur at all levels of the organization. So, we piloted this structure for administrator learning during the last two years and are formally launching Administrator Learning Teams (ALT's) across the system. Again, the staff — in this case, teams of administrators — determine their own professional learning as instructional leaders. And once again at the central office, we set the conditions to support this professional learning team model. Administrators have time to learn during the school day with coverage to attend to operational school issues as well as resources to support their inquiry or problem of practice. School-based learning time let us leverage the key conditions supporting continuous professional learning so we could turn on that bright light of learning across the system.

Clara Howitt, superintendent of education,
Greater Essex County District School Board
Windsor, Ontario

will get another black mark (Bill & Melinda Gates Foundation, 2014).

Yet, teachers are eager for opportunities to learn with colleagues and consider collaborative learning among the most meaningful forms of professional learning they can experience. Leaders in schools and districts have a responsibility not only to give sufficient time for learning but also facilitate a plan for using that time well.

Ultimately, teachers, with the support of principals and coaches, will be doing a delicate balancing act between the time they have allocated to work together and the work they plan to complete during learning cycles to achieve their learning goals. They're already working in predetermined multiweek grading periods and they're making choices about which goals to prioritize so that they may advance their students as far as possible by year's end. The learning team cycle of continuous improvement guides teams so they use allocated time in ways that lead to changes in practice and student results. When the learning team focuses their work specifically on the curriculum and instructional materials in use in their classrooms, they are in a position to apply learning immediately in service of students.

References

American Society for Quality (ASQ). (n.d.). Continuous improvement. Available at http://asq.org/learn-about-quality/continuous-improvement/overview/overview.html

Bill & Melinda Gates Foundation. (2014). *Teachers know best: Teachers' views on professional development.* Available at http://k12education.gatesfoundation.org/wp-content/uploads/2015/04/Gates-PDMarketResearch-Dec5.pdf

DuFour, R., DuFour, R., & Eaker, R. (2008). *Revisiting professional learning communities at work: New insights for improving schools.* Bloomington, IN: Solution Tree Press.

DuFour, R., DuFour, R., Eaker, R. & Many, T. (2010). *Learning by doing: A handbook for professional learning communities at work, Second edition.* Bloomington, IN: Solution Tree Press.

Hirsh, S. (2016). Michael Fullan affirms the power of collective efficacy. [Weblog]. Available at https://learningforward.org/publications/blog/learning-forward-blog/2016/04/20/michael-fullan-affirms-the-power-of-collective-efficacy#

Reflections

• We can describe the five-stage learning team cycle.
• We have ideas for how to enter the learning team cycle.
• We can describe some of our roles and responsibilities at different stages of the cycle.
• We can envision how to schedule learning cycles within the school year calendar.
• We can provide a rationale for using the learning team cycle to our colleagues.

Jolly, A. (2008). *Team to teach: A facilitator's guide for professional learning.* Oxford, OH: National Staff Development Council.

Lewis, C. (2014). Lesson study. In Lois Brown Easton (Ed.), *Powerful designs for professional learning, Third edition* (pp. 209–222). Oxford, OH: Learning Forward.

Michigan Department of Education. (n.d.). Instructional learning cycle overview: Continuous use of data to inform and differentiate instruction. Available at www.michigan.gov/documents/mde/ILC_Overview_415264_7.pdf

National School Reform Faculty. (2014, July). Cycle of inquiry for professional learning community activities. Available at www.nsrfharmony.org/system/files/protocols/smp_cycle_inquiry_plc_0.pdf

Ross, J.A. & Bruce, C.D (2007). Teacher self-assessment: A mechanism for facilitating professional growth. *Teaching and Teacher Education, 23*(2), 146–159.

Sagor, R. (2000.) *Guiding school improvement with action research.* Alexandria, VA: ASCD.

Wellman, B. & Lipton, L. (2009). *Data-driven dialogue: A facilitator's guide to collaborative inquiry.* Sherman, CT: MiraVia, LLC. Available at https://www.miravia.com/pdf/DDD_study_guide_final.pdf

Tools index for chapter 2

Tool	Title	Use
2.1	Understanding the five stages	Use this tool to develop a general understanding of the stages of the learning team cycle.
2.2	Reviewing the learning team cycle	Use this tool as a reference throughout the five-stage team learning cycle.
2.3	Creating purposeful team roles	Use this tool to help define or clarify team member roles and responsibilities.
2.4	Scheduling a learning team cycle	Use this tool to schedule activities in each stage of a 12-week cycle.

PART II

What are the stages of the learning team cycle?

CHAPTER 3

Analyze data

Where are we now?

We have the data we need to distinguish between the vision and current state.

STRONGLY AGREE   AGREE   NO OPINION   DISAGREE   STRONGLY DISAGREE

We know how to access the data we need to answer questions.

STRONGLY AGREE   AGREE   NO OPINION   DISAGREE   STRONGLY DISAGREE

We can accurately identify various types of relevant data.

STRONGLY AGREE   AGREE   NO OPINION   DISAGREE   STRONGLY DISAGREE

We are able to analyze and interpret multiple types of data to make decisions.

STRONGLY AGREE   AGREE   NO OPINION   DISAGREE   STRONGLY DISAGREE

Our data are helpful in guiding decisions and actions for each stage of the learning cycle.

STRONGLY AGREE   AGREE   NO OPINION   DISAGREE   STRONGLY DISAGREE

Overview

Teachers and school leaders have been pressed to use data over the last few decades, and that pressure is increasing. Yet, while *data use* has become a popular term among educators and politicians, evidence demonstrates that teachers and school leaders still struggle with making sense of data in the service of improved learning outcomes (Means, Padilla, DeBarger, & Bakia, 2009).

In this stage, team members analyze data so they can better understand their students and the challenges they are facing. When teams begin planning their data collection and analysis, they may also want to refer to Tool 2.2: Reviewing the Learning Cycle to identify the indicators they will need in this stage. They also may use Tool 5.5: Designing an Action Plan when they complete their analysis and begin to determine root causes. This chapter covers the importance of data to professional learning and the learning team cycle in particular. It focuses on how the learning team uses data to determine the greatest needs and to inform the goal-setting process. In addition, this chapter focuses on leadership strategies for building a team culture that embraces data-driven decision making and for developing the knowledge and skills team members need to use data effectively. Descriptions of the characteristics of a data-driven culture show the conditions in which teams may flourish. The chapter closes with the steps that learning teams take to access and examine data in developing a focus area for their work together and before setting learning goals for themselves and their students.

What are data?

The term *data* means "factual information (as measurements or statistics) used as a basis for reasoning,

discussion, or calculation" (see www.merriam-webster.com/dictionary/data). "In other words," write Guskey, Roy, and von Frank (2014) "data are what we know" (p. 2). They continue:

> By themselves, data are neither good nor bad; neither positive nor negative. Moreover, data have no meaning or intrinsic value when considered in isolation. They can be relevant or irrelevant, pertinent or immaterial. Data become meaningful and valuable only when processed, usually for the purpose of answering specific questions. (p. 2)

As discussed in Chapter 2 and described more fully in later chapters, teacher teams typically begin the learning team cycle with data analysis. While they progress through the cycle, they continue to use data to ensure they are on the right track toward achieving their outcomes. Data-based decision making is key to ensuring that a learning team sets the right goals, establishes the appropriate learning targets, and accurately measures progress. The following scenarios show succinctly how data analysis informs goal setting, professional learning, and future actions.

• • •

A team of 4th-grade teachers analyzes their students' results from state language arts assessments and local district writing samples and concludes that student organizational skills are weak. They decide to study standards that address writing organization. They complete two student writing assessments, score each others' writing, and discuss how to apply their learning to their teaching.

• • •

World history teachers analyze student essays and are disappointed that student work fails to demonstrate critical thinking. They decide that students would benefit from more explicit instruction in critical thinking. As a team, they identify four critical thinking skills and study how to teach those skills to high school students. They use lesson study to develop and refine a model lesson for each skill.

• • •

A group of algebra teachers reviews semester exam results and discovers that more than half of the students missed the same series of questions about one skill. After discussing the possible causes of this pattern, teachers decide that the method they used to assess the skill differed from the way it was presented in the textbook. They study the pros and cons of various methods of assessing the particular skill and determine how they want students to demonstrate an understanding of that skill in the future.

What is the relationship between data and professional learning?

The Data standard, one of the Learning Forward Standards for Professional Learning, describes the use of data in professional learning:

Data: Professional learning that increases educator effectiveness and results for all students uses a variety of sources and types of student, educator, and system data to plan, assess, and evaluate professional learning. (Learning Forward, 2011, p. 36)

The Data standard focuses on three elements: (1) educators analyze student, educator, and system data to determine needs; (2) educators use data to assess the impact of professional learning content and process; and (3) educators use data to report professional learning results. This chapter focuses on how the learning team uses data to determine their greatest needs and to inform the goal-setting process (see Tool 3.1: Understanding What It Means to be Data Literate to launch a discussion and promote shared understanding). In later chapters, teams will see that they use data throughout the cycle to support implementation and monitoring as well as to promote reflection and further planning.

Early in the cycle teams study data about students and educators to identify where students are in relationship to the standards and curriculum and to identify the most significant needs, which, in turn, will lead to team goals for professional learning and student outcomes. Team members use probing questions to identify potential root causes that can help to clarify the essential content for educator professional learning. Student data include multiple types such as daily classroom work, formal and informal assessments, and achievement data, including grades, benchmark exams, and end-of-course assessments. (Learning Forward, 2011, p. 36).

Knowing about student learning needs can guide teams in making decisions about educator professional learning, yet team members need more than just student data. Having a comprehensive understanding of educator learning needs is essential if teams want to plan for meaningful professional learning. To identify educator learning goals a learning team may consider various types of data, including the following: preparation information, performance on various assessments, educator perceptions, classroom or work performance, student results, and individual professional learning goals (Learning Forward, 2011, p. 37).

How do teams establish a data-driven culture?

Several conditions promote the effective use of data in driving improvement. School leaders who value data-driven decision making will create conditions in which all forms of data are accessible and valued and in which teachers can competently use those data to inform their practice (see Tool 3.2: Assessing Our Data Literacy for a rubric — an Innovation Configuration map that details knowledge and skills association with the data standard). In the vignette on page 39, read how one Maryland middle school principal collaborated with a local university to begin developing teachers' data literacy.

Make sure all forms of data are accessible and valued

Data from multiple sources enrich team decisions about professional learning that leads to improvement or increased results for every student. Multiple sources include both quantitative and qualitative data, such as common formative and summative assessments, performance assessments, observations, work samples, performance metrics, portfolios, self-reports. The use of multiple sources of data offers teams a balanced and more comprehensive analysis of student, educator, and system performance than any single type or source of data could (Learning Forward, 2011, p. 37).

Recognize that data analysis is an essential component of the improvement process

Without data teams lack guidance in choosing a direction. They may miss both the areas that require their attention and those that show their successes.

They may fail to fulfill commitments to ensure that all students and educators realize their potential. Educators who work within a data-driven culture seek out all available data. And they are able to select and deal with the data in a coherent way and without being overwhelmed. They do not proceed with goal setting or program adjustments without carefully examining data for the story it tells. Data analysis is not a separate element of the teaching and learning narrative; it is a component woven throughout that narrative (Jimerson, 2013).

School leaders have a responsibility to support the integration of data use into professional learning and to ensure that teachers have access to and skills to interpret data to improve curriculum implementation, instruction, and assessment. Teams are less likely to value the significance of data without the leader's guidance, direction, instruction, and support.

If leaders do not provide adequate support, however, teams may need to assemble the available data that will help them make their decision. Supportive school leaders view decision making without data as a waste of time — investing in data analysis is their priority.

Provide for safe data discussions

Successful teams adopt norms that ensure the privacy of their conversations and eliminate fear of reprisal for admitting where they need help. They want every team member to be comfortable in examining all aspects of the data. This may mean that data analysis reveals that students in one classroom perform better on particular learning outcomes than students in another. At this point, it is important for team members to feel comfortable in acknowledging their challenges and asking for help from their colleagues whose students performed so well. Team members must know that conversations at this level will not be shared beyond the group and will never be used to affect high-stakes employment processes.

Use data to support decision making

Data are everywhere and there is no shortage of them. Teams need to be able to use multiple data sources, rather than relying on a single data point to reach a deeper understanding of student learning. Team members conduct data analysis to clarify the gap between the desired vision and the current state and to inform specific educator and student learning goals for closing the gap. Later in the process, they will collect data to track their progress on specific outcomes and standards.

In a data-driven culture team work is aligned with the vision and priorities of the school system and their school. Adequate resources are allocated toward data-driven decision making. The most important resources necessary for effective decision making include the following:

- Team members know where to go to find the data they need most and how to access it.
- Team members know how to get help when they do not feel they have the skill set required for data analysis.
- Team members advocate, locate, and protect time necessary for their data decision-making tasks.
- Team members are comfortable in seeking outside expertise for assistance with data collection and/or analysis.

The ultimate goal is that the entire team shares deep expertise so that everyone feels equally competent to implement this important stage of the process.

Develop teacher expertise to make data-driven decisions

Effective, data-driven decision makers are data literate. Data-literate members of teacher learning teams will each be able to explain data sources, analyze and interpret data, and defend data decisions. After all, having a commitment to using data or even having access to available data do not guarantee that educators can translate those data into information that will help them make better decisions regarding future goals and professional learning. School leaders must ensure that all team members are data literate so that they may succeed during the data stage. Likewise, team members share the responsibility to work with colleagues, team, and school leaders to develop their own data literacy skills. The following descriptions suggest some key areas of expertise that are required of team members.

Determining which data to access

Team members need the skills to select the most appropriate data sources for the decisions they must make. Data-literate teachers must understand all types of data, such as assessment data. They need to be able to distinguish among different assessments and determine the best uses of the data they generate. Figure 3.1 shows a sample from one district of various assessments and their purposes as well as the data they generate to inform decision making. Data-savvy team members will know the differences between qualitative (e.g. focus groups, interviews, student work analyses) and quantitative (e.g. benchmark exams, norm- and criterion-referenced tests) data and their respective strengths and weaknesses. Many teams are fortunate to work in school systems that have data warehouses that organize data from multiple sources (e.g. norm-referenced tests, student work samples, student portfolios, and school system-designed tests) and make it accessible to all staff.

Data analysis paralysis

Collecting and analyzing data can be seductive. Many years ago, I was working with a team that loved studying data. They spent considerable time analyzing trends and patterns. They created comprehensive data walls that followed the performance of each student. They could describe in detail information on the status and progress of every student. And they were frustrated. After all their work, student performance was not improving. Unfortunately, they did not recognize their work had stalled at one phase of the cycle. They needed some help in recognizing what had happened as well as guidance for moving forward. Analyzing data for the sake of analysis does not move the work forward.

— Stephanie Hirsh

Making observations, inferences, and hypotheses about the data

Team members need the knowledge and skills to analyze and interpret data to make team, grade-level, department, and individual decisions about professional learning. The team has the expertise to make predictions, observations, and inferences from both qualitative and quantitative data. They use the data to decipher trends, patterns, outliers, and root causes within the data. Following the completion of this process they are better prepared to target the goal that will lead them closest to the desired outcomes and vision (Learning Forward, 2012).

Taking action

The previous section lays a foundation for building the data-driven culture essential to launching the learning cycle. During the data analysis stage, teams work through four steps to assemble and sort essential data so they can organize them; examine the data to identify performance trends, concerns, and opportunities; understand root causes; and write statements summarizing what the data tell them. All of this work, informed by data, deepens their knowledge about the state of student performance in their classes or across grade levels. They finish with data summary statements they can use to inform goal setting in the next stage.

1. Identify and collect essential data

Ideally, every team resides within a school and a system that has a vision for students. Throughout this book we imagine that teams plan their cycles around units. As stated earlier, the length and complexity of units will differ depending on the course or grade level. The amount of time a team has to spend on each stage will also determine how deeply they are able to go within each stage. While school systems have an abundance of data, learning teams need the data most relevant to the unit of focus.

However, all teams will benefit from broader data analysis to determine which units demand their attention. This decision can be guided by a school improvement plan and the data analysis that contributed to the schoolwide goals. For example, if a school has identified problem solving or academic language as a consistent problem across grade levels, grade-level teams may choose to focus their learning time on the units where these outcomes are targeted. Absent direction from schoolwide goals, the team may review data from last year's students as well as performance

Figure 3.1: An example of one district's different assessment measures and the data each generates

Standardized assessment	Benchmark assessment	Common assessment	Classroom assessment
Purpose: A standardized test is designed to measure the amount of knowledge and skill a student has acquired and produces a statistical profile used as a measurement to evaluate student performance in comparison with a standard or norm.	**Purpose:** A benchmark assessment is designed as a measurement of group performance against an established set of standards at defined points along the path toward standard attainment, typically administered every nine weeks.	**Purpose:** A common assessment is collaboratively developed by grade-level teams or departments as a measurement of group or individual performance against an established set of standards.	**Purpose:** Classroom assessment refers to all assessment activities undertaken by teachers, and by the students themselves, which provide information to be used as feedback to modify the teaching and learning activities in which they are engaged.
Designed by: Georgia Department of Education and national assessment vendors.	**Designed by:** Forsyth County Schools and state and national item banks.	**Designed by:** Collaborative teacher teams/departments.	**Designed by:** Classroom teachers.
Instructional data: Standardized tests can provide information on individual or group performance to help educators identify instructional needs, measure growth over time, evaluate effectiveness of programs, and monitor schools for educational accountability. Standardized tests are used at the national, state, system, school, and classroom level.	**Instructional data:** Benchmark assessment results can be used to determine student growth and student performance relative to grade-level and/or course achievement expectations. Results can guide classroom instruction and identify individual student needs for reteaching intervention, and/or acceleration. In addition, benchmark assessments provide periodic evaluation of program effectiveness and guide professional development efforts. Benchmark assessments are used at the system, school, and classroom level.	**Instructional data:** Common assessments can provide teacher teams with data to determine student performance relative to learning goals identified in a unit of study. Results can be analyzed to guide classroom instruction and identify individual student needs for reteaching, intervention, and/or acceleration. Shared results foster collaboration to improve instruction and embedded professional learning. Common assessments are used at the school and classroom level.	**Instructional data:** Formative assessment evidence is diagnostic and used to adapt the teaching to meet the needs of students. Results can be used to guide instruction and identify individual student needs for reteaching, intervention and/or acceleration. Students and teachers can use self-assessment to determine levels of achievement, set goals, and identify strategies to meet those goals. Classroom assessments are used at the classroom and student level.

Source: Tool 10.10: Striking a Balance in *Becoming a Learning School* by Joellen Killion and Pat Roy. Copyright 2009 National Staff Development Council.

Teachers' data dialogue creates ownership for professional learning

Years ago I observed the following as I facilitated a school improvement team meeting. We were at the data analysis phase and examining the results from our Reading Recovery intervention. To be honest, we were studying the data and attempting to organize it to make a case to the school board that we needed a third Reading Recovery specialist in our school. An amazing thing happened that evening: While everyone was deeply invested in pulling success stories from the data, the 1st-grade team of teachers was having its own conversation. A few days later, the teachers approached the principal with a request. By examining the data, they recognized how Reading Recovery had served so many of their students and the long-term impact it had for those students.

They also saw that the students who hadn't received Reading Recovery and had struggled in 1st grade, continued to struggle in 3rd and 4th grades. Those students probably would have benefitted if they had been served by the specialists. The teachers decided they could no longer wait for another specialist. They shared a personal obligation to develop the same knowledge and skills as the specialist so they could apply them in the classroom with all their students. Had they not engaged in the data analysis and discussion, these teachers might never have decided to advocate for an investment in their own professional learning. Backed by the data and a commitment, they asked for support so they could all receive Reading Recovery certification to reach and sustain success for more students.

— Stephanie Hirsh

of their current students the previous year to determine areas of greatest need.

When a team enters the learning cycle, they will access the curriculum and instructional materials available to them. They will begin by reviewing the goals set for the unit or time period. Recognizing that they will not be able to plan every lesson together, they will prioritize areas within the unit that will benefit most from their joint attention. Learning teams may begin the process by taking individually the end of unit or other available student assessments to provide background and insights into areas requiring their attention.

The following questions may assist team members in identifying additional data they could use to set and prioritize goals and a learning agenda in later stages:

- How did our students perform on the preassessment? (What do our students already know and what they are able to do with regard to the unit outcomes?)
- How did last year's cohort of students perform on the unit assessment?
- Which outcomes, content, and skills within the unit are most challenging to teach?
- What do anecdotal or observational data suggest about student needs?

This data discussion will enable the team to determine those lessons and areas that will require their greatest attention. The learning team determines together potential sources for answering the questions. They may assign different members the responsibility for collecting those sources.

Middle school-university partnership focuses on improving teacher data literacy to meet student needs

For the past two years at Elkridge Middle School, we've been learning to apply data to our improvement cycle. The leadership team is committed to making the process work so we've worked in partnership with Towson University. We've received coaching, support, and facilitation as staff have learned to collect, analyze, and apply data to teacher decision making about learning needs. We began learning how to conduct learning-based dialogues with data as a way to help lighten the load for teachers who had to implement a new evaluation process that included setting and monitoring progress on Student Learning Objectives. Staff had been willing to buy in because the data dialogue process would help them achieve their evaluation goals. As we began the process, however, we found that talking about instructional data turned out to be like letting strangers view the contents of your medicine cabinet: It made people uncomfortable. Reviewing data requires ownership of your instruction and the results. It means that if a student is not doing well in your class, you can't blame the student. You must examine the instruction.

The teams began by examining the assessments they use to ensure that they understand the terms included in the data report. Next, they developed focus questions: What was your lesson objective for the week? What data did you collect data to assess student mastery and what do the data show? They examined patterns of students' strengths and weaknesses shown in the assessment, and decided what action they would take based on those patterns. Team members have deepened their observations and inquiry as they have used data analyses and dialogues to recognize that student performance is related to the quality of their instruction. Conversations have shifted from "I expected more students to do better on that assessment"

Elkridge Landing Middle School	
Founded	1995
Student enrollment	734
Neighborhood	Elkridge, MD, Howard County
Demographics:	
Asian	13.2%
Black	14.9%
Hispanic	6.1%
White	57.5%
Free or Reduced-Priced Lunch	10.4%
English Language Learners	0 (<10)
Special Education	7.3%
Attendance	95.0%

to questions such as, "How could I have taught that lesson differently?" Teachers also have developed a more appropriate understanding of pacing guides. They realized that a pacing guide is simply that — a guide. Depending on student data, teachers more often made decisions to retest, review a lesson, or even reteach it, so they could to make sure that every child mastered the content. In considering differentiation for students, the team members adapted not only whole-class instruction, but also instructional supports like drill and homework to give each student additional instruction or enrichment based on his or performance.

During the 2015–16 school year, we began focusing more broadly on school improvement, using the rules and guidelines of data dialogue to guide our work. We continue to focus on data collection and analysis to determine differentiation strategies for students. But we still have a long way to go in clearly defining the interventions and strategies that classroom teachers can implement and those that are specialized interventions. At this point we've made progress in using data to talk about student learning; nevertheless, we will need more practice before teachers can act independently with the protocols.

Brenda J. Conley, clinical assistant professor Instructional Leadership and Professional Development, Towson University, Towson, MD

Gina Cash, principal, Elkridge Landing Middle School, Elkridge, MD

Because teams won't have time to focus on every single need, they need to look for the areas that are common across the team and would benefit most from a team focus. After they identify those areas, they set priorities and make the most of the time they have together.

2. Organize and display data for analysis

Many teams find it helpful to take the data and translate them into charts, graphics, or formats that paint a picture of the status of student performance. They may decide to disaggregate data according to the characteristics of the student body that are most pertinent to the team's planning. A learning team may begin, for example, by organizing student data according to gender, race, socioeconomic status, English language learners, and special populations. Or they may arrange the data according to outcomes as well as by classroom.

Not all teachers and support staff who serve the team's students are necessarily participants on the learning team. A member of the team may interview these educators to get their perspectives on the team data or invite them to a learning team session to share their observations. The team may also find it useful to have the support of the principal or a particular data expert or lead teacher as they do this work. Organizing and displaying data will be valuable when determining where to focus professional learning in the future.

3. Examine data for trends, issues, and opportunities

This is the time for the team to dig more deeply into the data to ensure that all team members can reach all students and surface all issues. At this point, team members will analyze their multiple sources of data to review current performance, describe performance trends, and identify root causes.

To help with the analysis process, teams may consider the following questions to guide examination of and discussions about the data. Depending on its specific context, a learning team will choose the most appropriate among the following questions:

- What do we know about the lowest-performing students?
- What do we know about the highest-performing students?
- How do boys and girls perform?
- What relationships do we see between students' performance and socioeconomic groups?
- Where do students struggle most?
- What can we learn from last year's students about their performance on these outcomes?
- Where were students most successful last year? Where did they struggle most?
- What patterns across classrooms do we see on different outcomes?
- What insights do we gain about the team members' particular strengths in teaching any of the outcomes?
- What concerns arise regarding our knowledge, skills, practices, and beliefs necessary to address our students' greatest weaknesses in these areas?

Because most performance problems are symptoms of other issues, the team tries to get a handle on a root cause of a performance gap. One definition of the root cause is a "statement describing the deepest underlying cause, or causes, of performance challenges, that, if dissolved, would result in elimination, or substantial reduction, of the performance challenge(s)" (Clark County School District, 2012, p. 9). Identifying a root cause will put the team on strong footing to move forward with future action planning and goal setting (see Tool 3.4: Crafting Data Summary Statements to support data analyses and then follow with Tool 3.5: Understanding Root Causes to help narrow and determine causes).

4. Summarize the data

Once they have dug deeply into the data, team members will translate the findings into summary statements or needs statements. During this step they will describe in a statement or more what the data tell them. The process of crafting data summary statements works like this: The team writes one or more summary statements, depending on the number and range of observations. Team members will write statements about the performance challenge specifying priority student subgroups and describing student needs with some detail. For example, a statement may contain information for cohorts of students within a grade level over time, within a disaggregated group of students, or within a content strand (e.g. reading comprehension in language arts). The language ultimately will inform the team's planning.

Each statement speaks to the data rather than assumptions about what members of the group think they say. At this point, your team avoids discussing potential solutions. Instead, these statements give potential guidance for setting learning and improvement goals.

Examples of such statements might include:

- Across all sixth-grade classes, 72% of girls are proficient in problem solving, while 64% of boys are proficient in problem solving.
- One out of four 5th-grade classes achieved the district's benchmark on the social studies six-week benchmark last six weeks and they continue to struggle with the higher-level thinking skills.
- Less than one-third of English Language Learners demonstrated proficient academic language use during the last grading period.

Reflections

• We collect data to determine gaps between our vision and current state. We know what information is available to define our desired state and we know where to find it.
• We know what types of data we will need to access regularly to define our current state and we know how to access them.
• We are confident that we have the skills and knowledge to interpret and use data to guide decisions about learning and improvement.
• We can create a safe environment for analyzing data so team members are comfortable discussing potentially difficult topics.
• We know what data we will regularly collect to inform our current learning and improvement process.
• We know how to use protocols to support the data analysis stage.

References

Clark County [Nevada] School District. (2012). School improvement planning basics: Root cause analysis. Las Vegas, NV: Department of Assessment, Accountability, Research, and School Improvement. Available at http://ccsd.net/resources/aarsi-school-improvement/pdf/planning/school-improvement-planning-basics-root-cause-analysis.pdf

Guskey, T., Roy, P. & von Frank, V. (2014). *Reach the highest standard in professional learning: Data.* Thousand Oaks, CA: Corwin Press.

Jimerson, J.B. (2013, October). Weave data into learning. *JSD, 34*(5), 50–53. Available to members at http://learningforward.org/docs/default-source/jsd-october-2013/jimerson345.pdf?sfvrsn=2

Learning Forward. (2012). *Standards into practice: School-based roles. Innovation Configuration maps for Standards for Professional Learning.* Oxford, OH: Author.

Learning Forward. (2011). *Standards for Professional Learning.* Oxford, OH: Author.

Love, N. (2002). *Using data/getting results: A practical guide for school improvement in mathematics and science.* Norwood, MA: Christopher-Gordon.

Tools index for chapter 3

Tool	Title	Use
3.1	Understanding what it means to be data literate	Use this tool to promote a conversation on the importance of data literacy among team members.
3.2	Assessing our data literacy	Use this tool to determine current strengths and potential areas for growth about how to use data for planning and decision making.
3.3	Finding data sources and developing a data plan	Use this organizer to inform a process for identifying and organizing data sources and developing a plan for data analysis and study.
3.4	Crafting data summary statements	Use data and the worksheets in this tool to develop a data summary statement that supports data analyses.
3.5	Understanding root causes	Use the brainstorming process and fishbone diagram in this tool to identify, narrow, and better understand causes.

CHAPTER 4

Set goals

Where are we now?

We write student and professional learning goals as a result of careful analysis of student and educator data.

STRONGLY AGREE | AGREE | NO OPINION | DISAGREE | STRONGLY DISAGREE

We begin our goal-setting process by studying our data summary statements.

STRONGLY AGREE | AGREE | NO OPINION | DISAGREE | STRONGLY DISAGREE

Our student and professional learning goals align with our system and school improvement goals and instructional frameworks.

STRONGLY AGREE | AGREE | NO OPINION | DISAGREE | STRONGLY DISAGREE

Our educator learning goals identify clearly what improvement we want in our knowledge, attitudes, skills, aspirations, and behaviors.

STRONGLY AGREE | AGREE | NO OPINION | DISAGREE | STRONGLY DISAGREE

Our student learning goals are written in SMART goal format and identify clearly what students will know and be able to do as a result of our changed practices.

STRONGLY AGREE | AGREE | NO OPINION | DISAGREE | STRONGLY DISAGREE

Our goals guide us toward the appropriate team learning models.

STRONGLY AGREE | AGREE | NO OPINION | DISAGREE | STRONGLY DISAGREE

Overview

Chapter 3 ended with the creation of data summary statements from which learning team members develop learning goals for their students and themselves. Disaggregating and analyzing data are necessary processes for identifying and understanding learning problems, but they are not sufficient for overcoming challenges. The learning team members need to translate findings into goals for their own learning and student performance. During Stage 2: Set Goals, team members get smart about choosing which gaps they will work to close from those they had identified in the first stage of the cycle.

This chapter shows how teams develop student and educator learning goals. Teams may turn again to Tool 2.2: Reviewing the Learning Cycle to check the indicators they will need in this stage as well as to make sure they have necessary resources and support for setting learning goals for their students and themselves. They also may use Tool 5.5: Designing an Action Plan when they begin to develop goals and complete a plan. The discussion presents a collaborative process for translating a team's data findings into goals that can be used to guide collective learning and actions as well as to establish expectations for overcoming the problems identified by the data. The team will later review these expectations in Stage 5.1: Monitor, assess, and adjust practice. Meanwhile, during the goal-setting stage, team members examine the instructional framework, curriculum guides, and testing schedule as they translate their data findings into a manageable number of goals on which to focus student and educator learning. Examples of learning goals show one format that learning teams can use to craft specific, outcomes-oriented, measurable goals for which they can be accountable in a timely fashion. This book suggests that teams use the SMART format for student learning goals. Then, in setting educator learning goals, team members identify the particular knowledge, attitudes, skills, aspirations, and behaviors (KASABs) educators need to develop to achieve those student goals. Regardless of the goal format a team, school, or district chooses, the key to successfully managing the goal-setting process is to keep in mind that the format of the goal is less important than the focus. Team members can manage the demands of this stage if they remember, first, to identify their greatest student learning needs and, second, set their own learning goals as a complement to student learning goals.

How do teams set the right goals?

Clarify outcomes

Chapter 3 highlights the importance of the Data standard as a benchmark for conducting data analysis. The standard provides a strong rationale and elements of effective data analysis to guide professional learning and student growth. For setting goals the Outcomes standard gives a similar rationale and guidelines for paying attention to both student and educator performance expectations:

Outcomes: Professional learning that increases educator effectiveness and results for all students aligns its outcomes with educator performance and student curriculum standards. (Learning Forward, 2011, p. 23)

Learning Forward's Standards for Professional Learning further explain the importance of focusing on both student and educator learning goals:

Student learning outcomes define equitable expectations for all students to achieve at high levels and hold educators responsible for implementing appropriate strategies to support student learning. Learning for educators that focuses on student learning outcomes has a positive effect on changing educator practice and increasing student achievement. (Learning Forward, 2011, pp. 49–50)

The standard reinforces the importance of aligning team goals with curriculum and performance priorities. After analyzing data to understand a number of issues affecting student performance, learning teams set goals related to student and educator learning outcomes that guide them toward achieving intended results.

Translate data into student goals

In "The X Factor is 'Why,'" Anne Conzemius (2012) says that educators use data as part of their ongoing professional practice to gain perspective on a problem, create focus and monitor progress, and to generate new learning (p. 21). In Chapter 3 the team concluded the data stage by writing data summary statements. These statements summarized the gap between the *desired* state and current state of student performance. In practical terms, a team may use the statements to describe the desired state as it may relate to system, school, or team aspirations. Translating student and educator data into useful data summary statements is only meaningful if it leads to well-informed action that achieves better results. The data show where students *are*. In goal setting, educators look at where they want students *to be*. And along with defining student expectations, educators think about where they need to be in terms of their own learning.

Anne Jolly (2008) offers a reminder that well-formed instructional goals create a sense of purpose among team members:

The learning team accomplishes good things for students because teachers focus their collective energy on an instructional goal

that addresses specific student needs. Teams without a clear goal may meet faithfully and share, swap, and exchange information and activities, but their lack of purpose, generally, guarantees that they wind up nowhere in particular.

A strong sense of purpose and a clear goal also keep teams on track. Daily brush fires and competing responsibilities coupled with the demands of teaching tug at teachers' energy levels and compete for their time. . . . Concrete, targeted goals, along with short-term milestones, give teams the sense of accomplishment they need to maintain teachers' energy level and motivation. (p. 53)

Discussing data statements should lead a team first to be able to answer the question, "What student learning gaps are most urgent as we look at our vision, curriculum, and instructional priorities?" Team members then use the answer to this question to inform the student goal that will guide the remaining stages of the cycle. Next, the team begins to answer the question: "And how will we know?" Forming clear answers to this question is a critical step to writing clear goals that will lead to well-aligned assessments and lessons (see Tool 4.1: Deciding on a Team Focus for a resource to prepare for setting learning goals for students and educators).

The following example shows how to move from data summaries to goal setting. Here is one of the summary statements at the end of Chapter 3:

Across all sixth-grade classes, 72% of girls are proficient in problem solving, while 64% of boys are proficient in problem solving.

The gap shows that a subset of students, namely boys, are lagging behind in this area. As the team considers how to frame its goal, it is building its plan to achieve one particular student learning target to close the gap revealed by the data.

Approaches to goal setting

Sometimes districts prefer or require that student goals be written toward specific approaches to goal setting: accountability, attainment, and growth.

Accountability

These goals focus on meeting an externally set level of performance as opposed to achieving proficiency or some level of improvement in their ability to solve problems. The following is an example of an accountability goal:

- 80% of our 6th-grade students will meet or exceed math standards in problem solving by the end of the first trimester.

Attainment

These goals dictate what and how students demonstrate attainment of a particular standard or competency at the conclusion of a period of study. Here is an example stated as an attainment goal:

- By the end of the first six weeks, all students will demonstrate 85% proficiency in using the most appropriate problem-solving technique(s) for solving a variety of challenges (or tasks) across content areas.

Growth

These goals dictate the acceptable percentage of improvement students demonstrate at the conclusion of a period of study. Here is a sample stated as a growth goal:

- By the end of the first six weeks, all students will demonstrate increasing levels of proficiency in problem-solving by using the most appropriate technique(s) for a solving a variety of challenges (or tasks) across content areas.

And some goals may contain elements of all three types.

After discussion, the initial student learning goal might be:

- All 6th-grade math students will achieve a proficient level or above on six-week benchmark assessments by selecting and applying appropriate strategies to solve grade and standards-specific problems.
  - Specific: problem-solving strategies
  - Measurable: benchmark assessment
  - Attainable: proficient
  - Results-oriented: grade and standards-specific problems
  - Time-bound: six weeks

In addition, the male students will demonstrate proficiency in each new problem-solving strategy on weekly assessments. The team assumes that if students strengthen their problem-solving skills, then they will improve in ways relevant to the gap identified in the data summary above. Checking progress on the weekly assessments addresses the gender performance gap identified in the data analysis. If males aren't making appropriate progress toward the benchmark, teachers may identify additional support and/or interventions.

The goal shows a strong orientation toward results with a specific outcome and it is measurable in more than one way. See sidebar, "Approaches to goal setting."

To read how one teacher team handled goal setting, see the vignette, "Goal-setting process stretches teacher teams," on page 51.

Create intentional educator learning goals

After reaching consensus on the student learning goal, team members must do the same for the educator learning goal. They will collaboratively identify what skills and knowledge they individually and collectively need to help students achieve this goal. Their learning goals answer the question, "What do educators need to know and be able to do to ensure students achieve their learning outcomes?" Responding thoroughly to this question keeps the team on the right track for success.

In too many cycles of inquiry or improvement, teams may collaborate to write SMART goals for students but skip the stage of writing goals for themselves. A deliberate focus on educator learning with intentional goal setting is what makes this learning cycle unique and particularly valuable for educators.

When teams do write their own goals, they will benefit from addressing more than educator knowledge and skills. In *Assessing Impact: Evaluating Professional Learning,* Joellen Killion (2008) outlines the various types of change that learning may impact. She introduces the KASAB model — knowledge, attitudes, skills, aspirations, and behaviors. By considering all elements within KASAB as they set learning goals, teams create the potential for transformational change in schools. If educators identify only the knowledge and skills they will gain, they ignore the importance of their beliefs, expectations, and behaviors in teaching and learning.

Knowledge and skills tend to be the elements of learning educators typically address. Knowledge, for example, might be understanding deeply the content of the next unit in the science curriculum. In scanning the content, the teacher recognizes that her own knowledge about a particular aspect of thermodynamics doesn't enable her to answer questions students may ask. To address this gap, she could turn to a resource or a peer for a reading or explanation and thus fill her knowledge gap. If she wanted to address her skill with that same aspect of the unit, she is concerned with how to teach the content and will explore research-based pedagogy appropriate for the content. Knowledge is the *what* while skill is the *how.*

The behavioral element of KASAB is what teachers put into practice — how they apply what they know in classrooms with students. A measure of the effectiveness of professional learning is often whether teachers take their learning and use it to change what they do with students. While they may hold the knowledge and skill in their heads about what to do, if they can't use the knowledge and skill to do something differently, their learning has fallen short.

Attitudes and aspirations are less immediately visible areas of learning. Attitudes are the beliefs educators bring to their work, both about their own efficacy and about their students' abilities. If a teacher believes he has no power to improve his performance or that of his students, that belief will afffect whether or how he changes. Yet it is possible to change beliefs. When teachers see evidence that they can improve, they change their attitudes about their efficacy. When teachers achieve success with students as they use new skills and practices, their beliefs about what their students can achieve shift. In the example of the science teacher preparing for a thermodynamics unit, she may hold a belief that she will do no better on that lesson in the future than she did last time. Once she recognizes that attitude, she may seek assistance in addressing it.

Aspirations are teachers' desires or motivations related to their work. When they hold aspirations to teach in ways that help all students succeed, they demonstrate those aspirations through rigorous expectations for all. Their aspirations are not only for their students but also for themselves. They want to improve so that all students will achieve higher outcomes. The aspirational element of learning, like attitudes, may be more difficult to articulate on a goal-by-goal basis yet they are important to call out in any scope of learning. The engagement of educators in this learning cycle process will over time have a significant impact on aspirations and attitudes; at the same time, their willingness to engage deeply in the cycle demonstrates their eagerness to improve.

In the following example of a teacher learning goal, team members directly connect to the student learning goal. The teacher learning goal will consider the knowledge, attitudes, skills, aspirations, and behaviors (KASABs) necessary to achieve the student learning goal. For example:

- By the end of the learning team cycle, team members will understand grade-specific standards, practice evidence-based problem-solving strategies, implement lessons, and use observation and evidence from student work to revise and improve instruction so that all students demonstrate mastery of the intended outcomes.
  - Knowledge: understand the grade-specific standards and problem-solving strategies
  - Attitude: belief that all students can use problem-solving strategies related to the unit
  - Skills: use new knowledge and student work to inform the process of designing, teaching, critiquing, reflecting, and revising instruction
  - Aspiration: want and expect all students to be able to use problem-solving strategies
  - Behavior: teachers and then students demonstrate application of grade and standard specific problem-solving strategies

As educators look for evidence of learning along each aspect of KASAB, changed practices are easy to observe. Shifts in knowledge and skill will be evident in the practices that are applied. Changes in attitudes and aspirations may be more difficult to detect but can be evident in teachers' persistence in addressing student misconceptions, their attention to every student's engagement, and their interest to learn other ways to approach instruction to improve results. Some of the tools that teachers use in Stage 4 will also provide indications of improvements in this area.

Right-size the goal

The cycle of learning is a continuous process; in the best case, educators can complete several cycles during the school year. Learning teams will start the year planning to complete a certain number of cycles according to the time allocated for their work together. They will also use the maps and pacing guides included with their curriculum, if available, as they identify how many learning cycles they will plan for the year. In some cases, the time allocated for teams is limited to a few days a year; those teams may only be able to complete one learning cycle. Teams that meet daily or weekly are best positioned to complete more cycles per year.

Although teams may begin the year by planning to address many goals together, they recognize that they may need to adjust their goals to the rhythm of the meetings and the rate of their progress. Limitations on their schedules will motivate teams to make choices among the range of student learning needs to address the highest priorities. While their time to learn together helps teachers schedule their cycles, so does the curriculum itself. As the year progresses and teachers and students move through the units or modules of their curriculum, they will be gathering data both about how well students are meeting overall goals for the year as well as how team learning cycles and goals align with everything they intend to accomplish.

Identifying goals of the appropriate size and scale requires teachers to make a variety of decisions. Informed by the data they've analyzed, teachers have already begun to consider particular target areas to address. As they examine the curriculum and instructional materials related to the target areas, teachers choose to identify goals at the unit level, the lesson level, or at the level of the student standard. In their decision making, they take into account their time to work together, the curriculum itself, and the learning need they are addressing. If, for example, they have very little time to work together, team members may believe they can achieve a goal that can be addressed in just one or two lessons. In that case, they may choose a lesson or two that offer particular challenges year after year. If their time allows them to work at the standard level, they may be addressing concepts that appear over several lessons, throughout a unit, or even across units. As teacher teams become more experienced in using the learning cycle, they will also become more skilled in crafting goals at a scale appropriate to their circumstances.

Use the SMART goal-writing format

According to Anne Conzemius and Jan O'Neill (2013), most educators state goals in terms of process rather than results. Process goals tend to "focus on the activities, programs, strategies, and methods that educators want to engage in. … Results goals answer the *so-what* question: So what if we did all these things? What actual improvement would we expect or want to see?"

> … Professional learning for teachers and principals is the means to achieve the goal of increased student achievement, so extend the traditional student achievement goal to include the end result of professional learning. (p. 244)

Today almost everyone is familiar with the "SMART" phrase, attributed to Peter Drucker's management-by-objectives approach some 60 years ago, although the term first appeared in a 1981 issue of *Management Review* in an article entitled, "There's a S.M.A.R.T. Way to Write Management's Goals and Objectives," by George Doran, Arthur Miller, and James Cunningham. New interpretations of the

acronym abound as educators use it to strengthen their goal-setting process.

Understanding how to apply these terms is a critical skill for writing powerful and compelling goal statements. The explanations that follow can help educators write powerful goal statements:

Specific goals focus precisely on the needs of students for whom the goal is aimed. And although "specific" is important, powerful goals are also systemic, strategic, and stretching. Team members have access to content standards and curriculum; they can collect and disaggregate data to identify commonalities and differences among student groups. Finally, they pinpoint areas for focus.

Measurable goals contain information about how much of a change will be made and how a change will be calculated or reported. Demonstrations, student work, and formative assessments all offer opportunities for meaningful evidence of results. The goal statement may even reference a particular tool or instrument that will be used to report results (e.g. portfolio or benchmark assessment).

Attainable goals include actions that the team can control or influence and that can be accomplished with existing resources. Goals must be achievable within the time period assigned to them. At the same time expectations must be high to inspire thoughtful action. The team also needs to strike a balance between goals that are too easy or too hard to reach in the time frame allotted. The team setting the goal identifies a baseline when determining whether a goal is attainable. The team also needs to know how much time and what other resources are available to accomplish the goal.

Results-based goals identify specific outcomes that are measurable or observable. Goals clearly state what students will know and be able to do. Results could be expressed as attaining a certain level of student achievement in a content area, an increase in the

> ### Student learning goal
>
> By the end of this unit, all 6th-grade students will demonstrate proficiency in the algorithm for long division, applying their understanding of place value, property of operations, and decimals.
>
> ### Teacher learning goal
>
> Team members will articulate their essential understandings of applying place value, properties of operations, and decimals to accurately use the algorithm for long division. They will solve math problems using base-ten diagrams to represent products and quotients of decimals to predict student approaches to the problems and prepare for potential misconceptions. They will engage students in these lessons during the upcoming six weeks, with appropriate adaptation or supplementation as needed to meet SMART goals. Team members will expect active student engagement and learning and will shift or adapt practices based on individual needs.

> ### Student learning goal
>
> By the end of six weeks, increase by 50% the 8th-grade Title I students who demonstrate proficiency and report increased efficacy in providing an objective summary of a text, including the theme and its relationship to the characters, setting, and plot.
>
> ### Teacher learning goal
>
> Team members will articulate essential understandings of and identify themes and their connections to characters, setting, and plot in readings. They will implement or adapt lessons in the curriculum to address particular needs of these students in the upcoming six weeks, with appropriate adaptation or supplementation as needed. Team members will expect active student engagement and learning and will shift or adapt practices based on individual needs.
>
> Source: Goals informed by our work with the Louisiana Dept. of Education, EngageNY resources, and expert input of colleagues at EdReports.org and CenterPoint.

number of students who improve in a certain area, or as improved performance as defined and measured by a performance rubric or clear criteria.

Time-bound goals identify the amount of time required to accomplish them. The goals are right sized according to the time allotted for achieving them. Goals are sometimes more compelling when there is a sense of urgency attached to them. A predetermined timeframe can create a sense of urgency and make the goal a priority to staff and students (Roy, 2007, p. 3).

In general, the SMART goal format gives learning teams a powerful tool to help determine which of their efforts is making a difference, encourage them to set benchmarks to monitor progress, and identify specific evaluation measures. While teams may choose — or be required — to set both teacher and student learning goals using the SMART format, the range of changes outlined in the KASAB model described above more fully address the many ways educators must grow. The sidebar shows a few examples of learning goals for students and teachers (see also Tool 4.2: Preparing to write SMART Student Learning Goals for additional resources on writing SMART goals).

Sequence educator and student goals

Student learning goals are essential to identifying teacher learning goals; however, teachers must act on their goals before they can expect to achieve the student learning goals. In their planning, teachers posit that if they were to gain certain knowledge and skills through intentional learning, their practice would shift and student learning would improve in specific ways. In other words, for teacher learning to shape student learning, teacher learning will precede student learning. Furthermore, unless teachers learn how to successfully apply their new learning to improve their instruction, they can expect little in terms of better results for students.

Goal-setting process stretches teacher teams

Teachers collaborate on goals that challenge students and themselves to deepen learning.

Dry Creek is one of 43 elementary schools in a large, diverse, suburban district outside Denver, Colorado. During the 2015–16 school year, the district began work to align professional learning community development across schools to deepen teachers' collaborative efforts. In service to this effort, the principal at Dry Creek partnered with a district professional learning specialist to support teams as they worked through the learning cycle

Teachers began by setting student learning goals that would guide their teams' collaborative work. Because teachers were already familiar with setting SMART goals, the teams set goals without much guidance, using primarily their grade-level standards to guide the goal writing. One example of a goal set by a primary team during this first draft was, "Eighty percent of students will use a period at the end of their sentences," a first-grade writing standard that the 1st-grade team determined to be an important one for students to master.

The principal and the district specialist crafted guiding questions that would challenge teams to consider how each stated goal would affect student learning. An example of a guiding question was, "Does the goal create opportunities for students to construct their own meaning and a willingness to engage in the process of meeting the goal?"

As teams used these questions to review the goals though a vertical lens, teachers began to notice that, if they achieved these goals, they would *maintain* rather than *push* the student learning status quo. Teachers realized they needed to review current student writing samples through a new lens. Applying the new lens led them to discover that their

Dry Creek Elementary School (Centennial, Colorado)	
Founded	1972
District/Area	Cherry Creek School District #5
Neighborhood	Suburban Denver
Student enrollment	420
Demographics:	
Black	3.2%
Hispanic	8.2%
White	68%
Other	20.6%
Free or Reduced-Priced Lunch	11%
English Language Learners	5%
Special Education	7%
Attendance	96.3%

goals reflected a learning outcome that students would easily achieve given current instructional practices. With this discovery, they initiated a process in which they revised their student learning goals. For example, when the team that initially wrote the punctuation-focused SMART goal reviewed their student writing samples, they saw that, in general, students understood how to apply the mechanics of writing, but were struggling to creatively express themselves. The team revised their goal to read: "One-hundred percent of students will communicate their intended message through focused writing that has a clear meaning." Reflecting the shared perspective of several of her colleagues, one team member said, "Looking at student data around *this* goal is much more engaging for me as a teacher than reviewing data about the punctuation habits of our students."

Now that the teams had revised the goals to reflect a meaningful, data-based vision for student learning, teachers could begin the process of writing goals around their instructional practices that were as challenging and rigorous as their newly crafted student learning goals.

Cherry Creek School District, Instructional Support Facility, Centennial, CO:

Tanya Batzel, professional learning coordinator

Kellie Randall, professional learning coordinator

This relationship is another reason that goal setting is so important: Advance planning for team and student learning is a critical step in achieving the outcomes.

Taking action

With an understanding of the key concepts underlying student and educator goal setting, teams are ready to work through the following steps to set student and educator learning goals:

1. Review summary statements and set priorities

Goal setting occurs several times a year. At the beginning of the school year, a school leadership team is typically writing year-end goals. These goals were informed by the leadership team analysis of previous years data as well as its own summary statements. These goals provide direction and have implications for grade level or subject matter learning teams.

When a team enters a new cycle, it will review the most recent summary statements before it begins the process of writing goals. A team will likely have many summary statements and find it difficult to prioritize among them. Hopefully, team members may feel as if they can address some of the issues raised in summary statements on their own without the added support of their colleagues. The data analysis and discussion of the problem may have led them to identify a practice they want to use or change immediately. They see these answers as "Nikes" — that is, they will just do it, as the action-oriented brand declares. Other summary statements are more challenging to address, and the team will agree they need to work on them together. When a team has too many summary statements, it may choose to use the school improvement goals to narrow its choices or ask an instructional coach or principal for guidance.

2. Write student goals

Teams translate their student goals into the SMART format (see Tool 4.3: Writing Student and Team Learning Goals for help in the process).

A previous discussion in this chapter covers an example of a student SMART learning goal.

When writing S.M.A.R.T. goals ask yourself:		
S	Specific	What will students and teacher achieve?
M	Measurable	How will it be measured?
A	Attainable	Are the goals realistic for students?
R	Results-based	Are the goals oriented toward clear outcomes?
T	Time-bound	Do we know when students will be expected to demonstrate attainment of goals?

The following is an additional goal with the SMART elements tagged:

- **Student:** By the end of the **fourth six weeks (T)** students will be able to **demonstrate appropriate use (M) of visual models (R)** including fraction bars, number lines, and area models **to correctly solve 80% (A)** of **problems requiring multiplication and division of fractions (S).** (engageNY, 2014, paras. 1–2)

3. Write teacher goals

In order to achieve student goals, teacher learning is required. KASAB is the framework teams may use to delineate all aspects of the teacher learning essential to successful student outcomes. There are three preliminary actions with guiding questions that learning teams can take to prepare themselves to write the most meaningful teacher goals:

- Scan the entire unit and instructional materials paying careful attention to the appropriate standards, objectives, lessons, assessments.

Reflections

- We can translate insights from data into priorities for student and team learning.

- We are clear on how to align student and team learning goals with our system and school priorities and curriculum.

- We write SMART goals for student learning.

- We can translate student learning goals into team learning goals that address knowledge, attitudes, skills, aspirations, and behaviors.

- We are competent in writing goals that provide guidance for learning and assessing impact of our work together.

- We right-size our goals in accordance with our curriculum and available time for team learning.

- We use feedback from others to strengthen our goal-setting process.

- What is the overall arc of the unit and materials?
- Where do the materials address the team's priority student learning goal?
- How comfortable are we with the guidance for addressing the goal?
- How do the assessments align with the goal?
- Dig deeply into the unit, lessons, and assessment with colleagues.
    - How do the models for learning provided in the lessons help students understand and achieve the targeted learning goals?
    - Could we complete the student assignments within each lesson?
    - Are we confident in our content and pedagogical expertise to implement the plan?
    - Could we demonstrate mastery on the outcomes at the conclusion of the unit based solely on the materials we have reviewed?
- Prioritize specific areas for further study and attention

- Which elements of the lesson(s) require additional learning and support for students and teachers?
- Are there prerequisite knowledge or skills our students may need to be successful?
- Will some students benefit from additional tiered support or enrichment?

After the team completes this process, it is prepared to address the KASAB elements covered in the example on p. 48. Following is a teacher goal with the KASAB elements tagged:

By the end of the learning team cycle, team members will understand grade-specific standards (K), practice evidence-based problem-solving strategies, implement lessons (B), and use observation and evidence (K,S) from student work to revise and improve instruction (K,S,B) so that all students (A, A) demonstrate mastery of the intended outcomes.

4. Review with others

Throughout this stage, especially, teams benefit from having strong relationships with individuals who can offer different points of view and support. During the goal-setting stage teams consider the perspectives of other teams, school-based coaches, principals, and district curriculum staff (see Tool 4.4: Checking Student and Team Learning Goals to review and finalize learning goals).

In summary, teams may think about making their goals public by sharing them with other teams, students, and parents. They may find it helpful to remember that high expectations yield higher outcomes. If members fall short on their goals, they must hold to their shared commitment and will to attain their goals. To do that they need opportunities to assess, adjust, and try again.

References

Conzemius, A. (2012, August). *The X factor is "why." JSD, 33*(4), 20–25. Available at http://learning-forward.org/docs/jsd-august-2012/conzemius334.pdf

Conzemius, A. & O'Neill, J. (2013). *Handbook for SMART school teams: Revitalizing best practices for collaboration, Second edition.* Bloomington, IN: Solution Tree Press.

engageNY. (2014, April). *Grade 6 Mathematics Module 2, Topic A, Lesson 1.* [Website.] Available at https://www.engageny.org/resource/grade-6-mathematics-module-2-topic-lesson-1

Georgia Department of Education. (2012, December). *Student learning objectives: Teacher quick guide.* Available at http://www.gadoe.org/School-Improvement/Teacher-and-Leader-Effectiveness/Documents/QG_Teachers%20SLOs%20for%20Teachers%204-1-2013%20FORMATTED.pdf

Jolly, A. (2008). *Team to teach: A facilitator's guide for professional learning.* Oxford, OH: National Staff Development Council.

Killion, J. (2008). *Assessing impact: Evaluating staff development, Second edition.* Thousand Oaks, CA: Corwin Press.

Killion, J. & Roy, P. (2009). *Becoming a learning school.* Oxford, OH: National Staff Development Council.

Learning Forward. (2011). *Standards for Professional Learning.* Oxford, OH: Author.

Roy, P. (2007). *A tool kit for quality professional development in Arkansas.* Oxford, OH: National Staff Development Council.

Tools index for chapter 4

Tool	Title	Use
4.1	Deciding on a team focus	Use this resource to support development of the team learning goal.
4.2	Preparing to write SMART student learning goals	Use this resource to gain additional perspectives on writing SMART format for student learning goals.
4.3	Writing student and team learning goals	Use this resource to guide writing of student SMART learning goals and teacher team KASAB learning goals.
4.4	Checking student and team learning goals	Use this tool to review and finalize learning goals.

CHAPTER 5

Learn individually and collaboratively

Where are we now?

We use our student and educator learning goals to guide our learning agenda.

STRONGLY AGREE	AGREE	NO OPINION	DISAGREE	STRONGLY DISAGREE

We apply the Learning Designs standard to the development of our learning agenda.

STRONGLY AGREE	AGREE	NO OPINION	DISAGREE	STRONGLY DISAGREE

We have processes and protocols for identifying content expertise and high-leverage learning models.

STRONGLY AGREE	AGREE	NO OPINION	DISAGREE	STRONGLY DISAGREE

We begin our learning by studying standards, curriculum, and units.

STRONGLY AGREE	AGREE	NO OPINION	DISAGREE	STRONGLY DISAGREE

We have processes for weighing collaborative and individual learning options and building a shared learning agenda.

STRONGLY AGREE	AGREE	NO OPINION	DISAGREE	STRONGLY DISAGREE

Overview

In this stage of the cycle, learning teams address the question, "How will we engage in learning to achieve desired outcomes for both ourselves and our students?" This chapter describes how a learning team decides what members will do to learn what they need to know so they can help students achieve their learning goals. It covers the importance of setting a learning agenda that guides team learning. Once again, Tool 2.2: Reviewing the Learning Cycle and Tool 5.5: Designing an Action Plan are resources that team members can use to check their progress during this stage as well as to make sure they have necessary resources and support for writing learning agendas and scheduling their own learning. Team members will also need to make sure that they agree on when and how some will pursue individual learning and when they learn collaboratively.

Why must teams pay so much attention to their learning?

Cognitive psychologists, neuroscientists, and educators have studied how learning occurs for nearly a century. The resulting theories, research, and models of human learning shape the underlying framework and assumptions educators use to plan and design professional learning. While multiple designs exist, many have common features, such as active engagement, modeling, reflection, metacognition, application, feedback, ongoing support, and formative and summative assessment, that support change in knowledge, skills, dispositions, and practice. (Learning Forward, 2011)

When educators fail to pay careful attention to teacher learning in schools, teaching and learning can stagnate. Only through learning will individuals

change and grow. This phase of the learning cycle is key to the team's achieving the vision they set and the goals they want for their students.

As teams choose among many collaborative and individual learning possibilities, team members home in on the outcome they seek. Having student and educator goals focuses the team; however, the goals do not define the learning or actions needed to achieve them. Team members decide for their learning agenda specific actions they will take to accomplish the goals on their learning agenda. To get to the point where they can create an actionable plan, the team first creates what Hirsh, Psencik, and Brown (2014) call a learning agenda, which is "an intentionally designed plan for learning to ensure that educators can understand and apply selected practices that improve their performance and student outcomes" (p. 130). By articulating their learning models and agreeing on their proposals, the team uses the learning agenda to "reflect on and learn from their own and others' experiences, and then create action plans to deepen their practice around what they are learning" (Hirsh, Psencik, & Brown, 2014, p. 130).

For the purposes of this book, a learning agenda:

- Restates the learning goals;
- Clarifies the content and process outcomes for educators;
- Identifies student curriculum units and assessments that align to the learning goals;
- Identifies the educator learning models to achieve outcomes;
- Schedules the adult learning.

The example discussed throughout the chapters of this book is a 6th-grade student learning goal focused on improving skills related to problem solving. The complementary teacher team learning goal focuses on increasing and improving explicit instruction in problem-solving strategies using ratio and rate reasoning (see Tool 5.1: Studying Learning Theories for Students to review the research-based framework and consider learning implications for lesson planning). To address the teacher team learning goal, the learning agenda may include the following:

- Scan entire unit and/or instructional materials, paying careful attention to the appropriate standards, objectives, lessons, assessments related to student and educator learning goals.

- Dig deeply into the unit, lessons, assessments with colleagues.

- Prioritize specific areas for further study and assess new understanding.

- Reflect on new knowledge and assess new understanding.

- Determine where new learning will be applied within unit and lessons and for enrichment and tiered support.

- Rehearse modified lessons.

- Refine lessons as necessary before implementation.

By the end of the stage, team members will be able to describe their new knowledge, skills, and behaviors, and develop an actionable plan for transferring their learning into the classroom with students.

Effective professional learning design is described in the Standards for Professional Learning

Decades of research have shown what it takes to design and implement effective professional learning. The Standards for Professional Learning codify those findings into practical summaries and advice for future action. The Learning Designs standard is particularly helpful in this stage of the learning team work:

Learning Designs: Professional learning that increases educator effectiveness and results for all students integrates theories, research,

and models of human learning to achieve its intended outcomes. (Learning Forward, 2011, p. 40)

Effective designs for professional learning assist educators in moving beyond a superficial grasp of a new idea or practice to developing a more complete understanding of its purposes, critical attributes, meaning, and connection to other approaches. Ultimately, the most powerful learning engages teachers in the same processes with the same content they intend to apply in their classrooms. To increase student learning, educator learning plans need to give educators many opportunities to practice new learning with ongoing assessment, feedback, and coaching so that the learned knowledge, skills, or dispositions become fully integrated into routine behaviors.

Honoring adult learning preferences

Designing a learning agenda is challenging work. Team members may increase their chances that everyone will be thoroughly engaged and successful when they consider principles of adult learning as they plan their learning. Adult learning theory has evolved since Malcolm Shepherd Knowles (1973) proposed his principles of andragogy. John Mezirow (1997) later showed that for adults to experience *transformative learning* — the process by which they change their frame of reference — they must experience something different in form from the learning commonly associated with children. Mezirow (1997) contended that ideal conditions of adult learning require that participants be free to engage in various roles of discourse, including becoming critically reflective of their assumptions and consciously planning and acting to bring about new ways of viewing their worlds (see Tool 5.2: Understanding Principles of Adult Learning for more information about adult learning).

In *Learning to Listen, Learning to Teach,* Jane Vella (2002) drew on research to describe twelve interconnected principles of adult learning. She argued that adult learning requires "participation of the learners in naming what is to be learned" (principle 1), a design that conveys to adult learners "this experience will work for them" (principle 2), and "respect for learners as decision makers of their own learning" (principle 6) (p. 4).

From Mezirow to Vella, then, emerges the theme that effective adult learning looks very different from what many teachers experience as professional development. Their constructivist theories are grounded in a body of research that shows people gain knowledge and meaning from the interaction between their experiences and beliefs. For real learning to take place, moreover, adult learners must become agents of their own learning (Calvert, 2016).

These learning preferences can also be influenced by a particular career stage of an individual, age of the learner, or his or her availability for certain kinds of activities. Some people are auditory learners and others prefer tactile learning; some like to read and others like to observe. Team may access different instruments (e.g. Myers-Briggs Type Indicator [MBTI], Kolb Learning Style Inventory [LSI], Visual, Auditory, Read-Write, Kinesthetic Learning Style [VARK]) to help members define their preferred learning style. Team members may use these frameworks and information to guide their selection of the final learning designs. After the team identifies appropriate learning designs, it can decide which ones must involve everyone and which ones allow individual choices.

New research findings may inform the learning agenda

During the past two decades, researchers have defined — and continue to refine — what is known about the conditions and characteristics of effective professional learning. Most educators know, for example, that effective professional development is planned over time, is sustained, collaborative, and embedded within the context of the school, and engages teachers in ways that cause them to develop their knowledge and skills in ways that improve student outcomes (Desimone, Porter, Garet, Yoon, & Birman, 2002; Goddard, Goddard, & Tschannen-Moran, 2007; Timperley, Wilson, Barrar, & Fung, 2007). With such active learning and intentional application, teachers can make instructional choices to meet student needs. As questions about the impact of professional learning continue to be raised and addressed, a growing number of important studies document the relationship between adult learning and student learning.

A recent report by Learning First, in cooperation with the Center on International Education Benchmarking, provides evidence that continuous professional learning deeply embedded into the framework of schools is fundamental to student success. In *Beyond PD: Teacher Professional Learning in High-Performing Systems*, Ben Jensen, Julie Sonnemann, Katie Roberts-Hull, and Amélie Hunter (2016) examine teacher professional learning practices and identify common patterns across four high-performing school systems: British Columbia, Hong Kong, Shanghai, and Singapore. Each of these systems implemented major education reforms that raised student success. Each also embedded concomitant professional learning into the routine daily work of teachers. The report provides a valuable summary document that details some significant professional learning studies and what we can learn from each. See Tool 5.3: Reviewing Summary of Evidence on Effective Professional Learning. Reviewing a few of these studies may help a team confirm for its members or colleagues the wisdom of investing time and other resources in this stage of the work.

Rather than merely calling for a single traditional workshop, the Learning Designs standard reinforces the importance of sequencing appropriate learning designs. The intended result is that teachers are able to effectively implement and adapt curriculum in the classroom. Effective planning for professional learning involves matching the most appropriate learning design to an educator's given need as he or she moves from developing new knowledge to practicing new skills to implementing a change with fidelity (Roy, 2013, p. v).

Early adult learning experts (Knowles, 1973; Mezirow, 1997) discussed how most adults change their practices not simply from reading and observing others work, but from combining multiple strategies. Education researchers continue to affirm that assertion. In his meta-analysis ranking the impact of different interventions, John Hattie (2009) found that professional learning activities such as formative assessment (ranked 3rd) and feedback (ranked 10th) had strong effects on student learning.

The discussions in this book center primarily around professional learning that improves teaching by developing teacher content knowledge and instructional practice. Research on effective professional learning describes several options for achieving this outcome so that learning teams can make considered choices (see Tool 5.4: Examining Learning Designs). Team members develop a learning agenda that will help them apply their professional learning to close gaps in their knowledge, skills, and practices.

What contributes to a powerful learning agenda?

While individuals may have experience in building their own professional learning plans, this book recommends an approach that intentionally integrates teacher learning and standards-based curriculum.

Research has demonstrated the importance and impact of a core curriculum on better outcomes for students. The learning agenda process is grounded in the assumption that the school system recognizes the importance of ensuring its teachers have high-quality curriculum and instructional materials to ground planning and learning. Absent these important resources teachers have to spend too much time securing and evaluating materials and have little time left for their own learning. When teachers don't have access to an effective and aligned curriculum, there are fortunately several organizations and websites that now support educators in evaluating materials for quality.

Team members have limited time to learn together. Once they arrive at this stage, they have determined the areas that require shared attention. Team members may have other individual learning priorities and are able to use other time and learning methodologies to address those learning needs. The learning cycle offers a fairly prescriptive protocol to guide learning for the team members. While some members of the team may feel it is too prescriptive, differentiated support will be available through individual learning plans; even within the team cycle there will be times when individuals seek varied sources or strategies for growth.

Setting student and educator learning goals

Effective professional learning plans are aligned to student and educator learning goals, as this book covers in the previous chapter. Clear student and educator learning goals focus the attention of the team on the areas they have identified as most important. Learning teams use the SMART and KASAB models to guide goal development. Learning teams also benefit from examining the instruments that are used to assess student mastery as part of their goal-setting process.

Grounding learning in the curriculum and instructional materials

Planning and implementing great lessons that ensure student mastery of required outcomes is a priority for every teacher. Integrating professional learning and curriculum and instructional materials ensures teachers the opportunity to focus on the specific work they will do with students in the classroom.

By grounding team learning in the curriculum, teachers learn or review critical pedagogical content knowledge that may not have been addressed in their preparation program. Or they may establish new and deeper connections to the content and their students. When they dig into units or modules, teachers see the arc of lessons and identify areas that may challenge students or themselves. As they study assessments team members may surface alignment challenges and other teacher learning needs.

Accessing expertise

Once a team establishes its most important learning needs, it will determine where to find the expertise required to fill gaps in knowledge, skills, or practices. Expertise often lies within the team and should be the first place to look. Ideally the data collection process surfaced where individual teachers have such expertise. If expertise does not exist within the team, then the next action may involve seeking support from an instructional coach, content lead, or principal. Once expertise is located the team will determine together the learning models it prefers for addressing its learning goals.

Figure 5.1 gives an example of a learning agenda framework to help align goals with learning designs (see pp. 61–63).

Figure 5.1: Learning agenda protocol

Example learning agenda framework*

To set a learning agenda, consider the example of a learning agenda framework on pages 61–63, which outlines steps and specific questions to address for each step. Presumably by this stage, learners have analyzed data and established learning goals for both educators and students.

For the purposes of this example learning agenda, consider the following student SMART goal and educator KASAB goal, which are examined for 8th-grade language arts:

Language arts

- **Example student SMART goal:** By the end of the first six weeks, increase by 50% the 8th-grade Title I students who demonstrate proficiency and report increased efficacy in providing an objective summary of a text, including the theme and its relationship to the characters, setting, and plot.

- **Example educator KASAB goal:** Team members will articulate essential understandings of and identify themes and their connections to characters, setting, and plot in readings. They will implement lessons in the curriculum to address particular needs of these students in the upcoming six weeks, with appropriate adaptation or supplementation as needed. Team members will expect active student engagement and learning and will shift or adapt practices based on individual needs.

* The learning agenda examples on the following pages are ambitious; learning teams will adjust the scope of their agenda to fit the size of the goals they set and the time they have to learn together.

Focus	Questions to address as you design learning agenda	Language arts goal learning agenda
Review		
Scan entire unit and/or instructional materials, paying careful attention to the appropriate standards, objectives, lessons, assessments related to our student and educator learning goals.	• What is the overall arc of the unit? • Where will the specific student learning goal be addressed? • How well do we understand the content essential to the student and educator learning goal? • How do the assessments appear to align with the goals?	• Read relevant units and materials, paying careful attention to those lessons that address summaries and themes.
Dig deeply into the unit, lessons, assessments with colleagues.	• How do the models for learning provided in the lessons help students to see/understand how to meet the targeted learning goal(s)? • If one completes the provided assessments, what evidence of student learning for the targeted learning goal(s) would be seen? • Can we complete the teacher and student assignments within each lesson? • What are potential student and teacher challenges and ways to address them? • If we were students, could we show the desired evidence of mastery of targeted learning goal(s) for the provided assessments with only the planned instruction in the unit/lessons?	• Discuss questions to the left, paying particular attention to those elements of the lessons that address the targeted content area(s).
Prioritize specific areas for further study.	• Which elements of the lessons require additional learning and support for students or teachers if we are going to achieve our goals? • What do we need to learn to help students who require tiered support or enrichment? • What do we need to learn to be responsive to our students who have a different cultural fluency than we do?	• Anticipate student challenges with analyzing how a theme is developed over the course of a literary text through changes in character, setting, and/or plot as well as the simultaneous expression of an objective summary of the literary text; • Understand how the selected text and use of two texts with similar themes but different development methods can support enriched, deeper learning of the targeted learning goal; • Determine where educators need further content and pedagogical support and understanding.

Figure 5.1: Learning agenda protocol continued

Example learning agenda framework*

Focus		Questions to address as you design learning agenda	Language arts goal learning agenda
Study			
Access expertise.		• Who has expertise in the areas we've identified, within or beyond our team? • What other sources of expertise can we tap? • What learning designs are appropriate for achieving our goals? • What perspectives might be missing as we think about where we gain expertise?	• Ask a team member with success in reaching this population to address core learning priorities; • Observe online or in person teachers who are successful with this population in other schools; • Practice with each other the scaffolds to the instructional materials as suggested in the teaching guide; • Practice applying the student outcome with literary texts whose themes speak to the benefits of diverse populations for society; and • Investigate concept of growth mindset.
Reflect on new knowledge.		• Did our learning challenge our understandings or assumptions? • How did our attitudes, assumptions, and aspirations shift as a result? • What new knowledge, skills, and behaviors do we have as a result of our learning?	• Reflect on what you learned from the various learning models; • Consider how they affected your knowledge, attitudes, aspirations for your students; • Identify, from what you observed, teacher actions that appeared to have the greatest impact on Title I students; and • Discuss opportunities for integrating selected changes in the unit.
Assess new understanding.		• Do we feel prepared to implement new learning? • Do we feel prepared to differentiate for students based on varying needs and cultures? • How do we perform on student assessments related to the areas studied?	• Work through formative assessments throughout unit; • Take next unit test as a learning team and grade tests; and • Create new and/or refine available formative and summative tools to assess change in student efficacy.

* These learning agenda examples are ambitious; learning teams will adjust the scope of their agenda to fit the size of the goals they set and the time they have to learn together.

Focus	Questions to address as you design learning agenda	Language arts goal learning agenda
Practice		
Pinpoint where new learning will be applied in unit and lessons; identify tiered support; revise lessons as needed.	• What will it look like when we teach the unit or lesson with the new knowledge and practices we've gained? • What will we emphasize within the unit lessons to meet our student learning goals? • For those students who do not have prerequisite skills, how can scaffolds and supports help them master the targeted learning goal(s)? • For students who come into the unit already with mastery of the targeted learning goal(s), what enrichment adaptations can support deeper learning? • Are these options available within the instructional materials or do we need to supplement? • In what ways are our planned supports culturally responsive to the students who need them? • How will our shifts in beliefs and aspirations be evident?	• Identify how to provide tiered support options within the unit and lessons; and • Highlight within each lesson what is most appropriate for target population and add tiered support where data indicate such choices are applicable, including any supplementation or adaptation needed.
Rehearse modified lessons.	• Which content or lesson segments would we benefit from rehearsing? • What evidence will we collect to support our perspective on the success of the lesson? • How well do our lessons appear to work?	• Practice teach a lesson segment with a small group of students and ask other teachers to observe.
Refine lessons as necessary before implementation.	• What changes in our lessons seem necessary? • What improvements will we make to be responsive to the varying needs and cultures of our students?	• Improve lessons after rehearsals.

Source: Adapted from https://www.engageny.org/resource/grade-8-english-language-arts and informed by our work with the Louisiana Dept. of Education and expert input of colleagues from EdReports.org and CenterPoint.

Reflecting on new knowledge and skills

Reflection is critical to addressing *Attitude* and *Aspiration* in the KASAB model and also useful for processing new knowledge and skills. While reflection can help team members recognize the shifts in their practice, it can also surface assumptions and strongly held beliefs challenged by the new learning and expectations. Reflecting on new learning overall, team members can elevate the changes they commit to making.

Assessing new learning

Assessing new learning and understanding ensures that team members have developed the depth of understanding required for the unit, module, or lessons. Deep understanding ensures educators are better prepared for the challenges they anticipated and that they can assist students who are struggling and those who will benefit from enrichment. Using student assessments is one useful indicator of educator readiness.

Integrating new learning in lessons

Depending on the goal and time allocated to team learning, the team determines which lessons to focus attention on. Team members re-read each lesson with an eye on their own understanding of the content, how they will teach it, and what student questions they anticipate. Based on the new learning, they make notes within the teaching materials to provide reminders of key ideas and explanations. They make references to supplemental explanations or strategies to enrich student engagement. They also identify and record activities for tiered support and enrichment. This level of team work ensures high-quality lessons for their students and reinforces new learning.

Rehearsing and refining enhanced lessons

Veteran teachers may recognize the situation that students in classes scheduled later in the day experience better teaching than those who have a lesson in the morning. While time may limit how much rehearsal team members can fit into their learning, such practice is incredibly beneficial to polishing lessons. Recent reports indicate that in other countries teachers have dedicated time to polish and rehearse lessons to ensure that students experience the best they have to offer. Hopefully, teams will not skip this step; once they have had a few opportunities to experience the benefits of rehearsal, they will become more invested in doing it in the future.

Rehearsal helps team members prepare for portions of lessons that are less familiar or more challenging. Practice lets team members determine how well their plans translate into the classroom. They experience the activities they will ask their students to complete, a key tenet of effective professional learning. They have advanced warning for areas that require attention and potential revision before the implementation stage.

Refine lessons as necessary. The learning cycle is about continuous improvement and there will always be ways to improve the work. The challenge to the team is when to "put pencils down" and be satisfied with the accomplishment to date.

Refining lessons should take place as quickly as possible following the demonstration. Waiting too long could mean that team members are unable to interpret their notes or remember how they were feeling at different segments of the lesson. Try to make sure that time for refinement is scheduled within the same time frame as the rehearsal. If this requires scheduling smaller segments, considering doing so. See Tool 5.5 Designing a Learning Agenda for questions to guide refinement and next actions for this phase of the work.

Taking action

In a learning system, leaders focus not only on individual learners, but also on the broader community of learners to which they belong. Andy Hargreaves and Michael Fullan (2012) remind us that an organization cannot increase individuals' strengths in isolation. One individual on his or her own cannot learn enough to ensure student success. Every effective team or community has potential to be a learning laboratory in which each person comes to understand and support the group's goals. Some teams appear to learn better than others; individuals may accelerate their teammates' learning by increasing their own awareness and adapting their behavior as needed. The group's resulting feelings of safety, trust, and intimacy determine how effectively team members learn on their own and bring that knowledge and understanding to bear on the team's collective learning.

High-performing learning teams thrive in learning systems and schools. By investing in the processes of individual and collaborative learning, teams enrich and extend a culture of learning. Even lacking a supportive learning school, they may be able to create their own learning culture. Learning teams may use the following steps to support ongoing learning and improvement for themselves and their students.

1. Set learning priorities

As the team set its goals, it reviewed the upcoming unit or module and considered what learning could be most challenging to students. It compared those considerations with its data to determine the goal(s) it would set for students. Once the team identified student goals, it considered the essential knowledge, skills, practices (behaviors), as well as attitudes and aspirations essential for teachers to guide students toward the intended outcomes. Looking back at the curriculum and/or instructional materials helped the team pinpoint the areas where the most help is needed.

Reread the relevant units, modules, and instructional materials thoroughly

Team members consider the overall arc of the curriculum and where the relevant units or lessons fall. They pay particular attention to specific references or guidance relevant to the student and educator learning goals. They consider educator competencies essential to the student learning goal along with the rationale for the proposed sequencing of lessons and activities. Finally, team members check alignment of the student assessments to the goal and lessons. After this careful review, team members are ready to tag potential areas for further study.

Dig deeply into the lessons

Team members imagine teaching each lesson (or engage in discussion of selected lessons closely tied to the student goals), completing as many student assignments/tasks as possible. This allows teachers to identify areas where they expect students to struggle and ways to address that. Reviewing the assessments at the end of each lesson gives teachers ways to consider whether the lesson design would lead to a successful outcome. Also important to consider are prerequisite skills needed by students and implications from those for team learning. Team members may also explore where tiered support and additional enrichment would be useful. Throughout this process, team members record what they anticipate will require further discussion, support, and learning.

Prioritize specific areas for further study

Given all the learning topics and needs, the team will prioritize the list and translate that into a plan for learning. Intentional learning around a few select issues or topics will strengthen teachers' capacity to deliver lessons in ways that accelerate student success. Ideally there is clear alignment between the student SMART goals, the educator KASAB goals, and the details and questions surfaced as priorities. If not, the team may need to do some work on one or the other.

2. Write team and individual learning agendas

During this step, teams write the plans that address how they will achieve the outcomes they established in their learning goals. There are three key actions they can take to support them in developing this plan.

Identify expertise

The team has set its learning priorities and needs to know how they will be addressed. Identifying expertise to support the learning is the first step in delineating a process that will lead to new understanding and practices.

Educators consider the following questions to help build the plan:

- Is expertise within the team or school?
- Is expertise elsewhere within the school system?
- Is expertise available through other professional learning networks, higher education institutions, or online resources?

Once teams have identified their sources of expertise, they determine how to gain the knowledge and skills they seek. There are a number of ways to gain new knowledge — readings, lectures, videos, and courses are typically widely accessible. However, being able to translate new learning to deep understanding and practice is much more challenging and requires

> ### Student learning goal
>
> By the end of this unit, all 6th grade students will demonstrate proficiency in the algorithm for long division, applying their understanding of place value, property of operations, and decimals.
>
> ### Teacher learning goal
>
> Team members will articulate their essential understandings of applying place value, properties of operations, and decimals to accurately use the algorithm for long division. They will solve math problems using base-ten diagrams to represent products and quotients of decimals to predict student approaches to the problems and prepare for potential misconceptions. They will engage students in these lessons during the upcoming six weeks, with appropriate adaptation or supplementation as needed to meet SMART goals. Team members will expect active student engagement and learning and will shift or adapt practices based on individual needs.

thoughtful consideration of learning designs. The most desirable involves engaging team members in learning settings equivalent to what they are expected to replicate in classrooms. Modeling teaching with learning team members or a group of students is a powerful way of addressing this. In the vignette on page 68, read how grade-level learning teams, using a modified lesson study design, reflected on videotapes of themselves teaching to plan for, practice, and assess their instruction.

Tool 5.5 may be helpful for recording your learning agenda.

Practice reflection

Intentionally reflecting on learning will deepen understanding and surface issues for further discussion. Individuals may benefit from individual reflection before engaging in team reflection. During the learning cycle, the following questions may be helpful in guiding both:

- What are the key new learnings?
- What are new or reinforced skills and practices we look forward to applying in the future?
- Where are we still struggling?
- What did we think about this issue before we investigated it more deeply? How have our views changed?
- Did our learning challenge or shift any of our other assumptions?
- What about our attitudes? How are we feeling about being able to achieve the goals we have set for this unit or module?

Tool 5.5 may be helpful for recording your learning agenda.

Assess educator learning

At this point team members check one more time to determine readiness for practice. While their reflections may indicate a sense of accomplishment with the targeted learning, assessment is important for checking understanding. Assessing the learning help educators know if they truly prepared for what comes next — transferring learning to practice. These questions can help with this task:

- How did we do on the student assessment? Do we need to review anything again?
- What are the big take-aways from the intentional learning?
- Do we feel prepared to implement the new learning?

LEARNING GOAL EXAMPLE

Problem solving for 6th graders

Returning to the sample student learning goal for 6th graders (see sidebar p. 66), one can see that the team might explore the curriculum and standards for place value, decimals, and properties of operations that 6th graders are expected to apply to their use of the algorithm for long division. They may also explore what evidence says are the most effective strategies for teaching the various strategies to 6th graders. During the research process team members may discover professional learning options that address their learning goals. They will certainly keep track of these options as they will be useful when they come to writing their learning agenda. Finally, team members will determine whether all members of the team must address all the goals. Team members may specify their highest priorities for learning among the various goals. However, if a team member does not want to opt into a team learning goal, he or she must produce evidence of competence related to the goal as well as previous student success in achieving the goal.

- How do we anticipate our practice will change?

Tool 5.5 may be helpful for recording your learning agenda.

3. Practice new learning

It has been said that practice makes perfect and training without follow up is malpractice. Equal attention should be paid to acquiring new knowledge

Elementary school opens up to collaborative professional learning

Becoming the host site for the Fairfax County Public School's (FCPS) Elementary ESOL Community of Learners was only the first step in changing how teachers learn at Centreville Elementary. When the district wanted to move the Community of Learners to the school six years ago, we seized the opportunity to create the conditions for real-time, embedded, collaborative professional learning. Using *collaborative learning* visits, the Community of Learners, the FCPS Office of ESOL Services, and Centreville provide a full day of job-embedded professional development for up to two grade-level collaborative teams from schools around the county each week. In opening our doors to these visits, the staff of this linguistically and ethnically diverse majority-minority elementary school began a journey that would transform our own professional learning.

As the faculty became comfortable with other teachers regularly observing in their classrooms, they began to interact with the visitors and embrace the job-embedded professional learning provided through the visits. So, when teachers asked to use the learning visit process themselves, we created our own collaborative learning visit protocol. But as much as we valued the reflective culture the visits brought to the school, we had limited funds to conduct this professional development as often as we wanted. Instead, with school reading and math specialists, the principal designed modified lesson study with video that would embed guided practice and reflection with the staff in their grade-level collaborative teams. And because of their experience with collaborative learning visits, teachers were able to shift from the visit process, which was closely guided by school leaders, into team-led modified lesson study supported by reading and math specialists.

In the modified lesson study format the team plans a lesson together; one teacher is videotaped teaching the lesson; the team follows a protocol to watch and reflect on the videotaped lesson together; they revise

Centreville Elementary School (Centreville, VA)	
Founded	1878
Student enrollment	927
Neighborhood	Region 4, Fairfax County
District/Area	18 miles west of Washington, D.C.
Demographics:	
Asian	28.48%
Black	8.63%
Hispanic	17.26%
White	39.16%
Free or Reduced-Priced Lunch	23.62%
English Language Learners	17.48%
Special Education	11.33%
Attendance	98%

the lesson and videotape a second teammate teaching it. The focus is not to evaluate the videotaped teacher, but to determine whether the team's planned lesson and strategies are effective in improving instructional practice. Because each teacher will be videotaped, team members are committed to actively participating in the lesson design and differentiation to meet the needs of all learners at the grade level.

With heightened sensitivity to student experience, teams have begun to assess lessons more from the student than the teacher perspective. One 5th-grade team immediately recognized that their minilessons were too long when they saw student engagement plummet after 15 minutes, largely because the lesson was lengthy and complex. The team had received similar feedback from the reading specialist in weekly planning sessions. But, they only recognized it when they watched the videotape and saw themselves and the plan through the students' eyes. Seeing reality on the tape has since led the team to change how they plan lessons. Centreville teacher teams have been able to direct their own learning with lesson study because they opened their classroom doors and came to value public, collaborative, and reflective practice.

Centreville Elementary, Centreville VA :

Dwayne A. Young, principal
Kelly H. Baugh, ESOL instructional support teacher
Amy Carey, reading specialist
Gretchen Polivka, math specialist

and skills as practicing new knowledge and skills in the team learning agenda. There are three key actions to guide this step.

Integrate new learning into lessons

The team returns to their unit or module and the lessons they intend to strengthen based on the new learning. As the team once more walks through the lesson(s) they address the following questions:

- How will the lesson potentially change as we teach it based on our new knowledge and skills?
- How can we strengthen the directions or guidance given to students to support greater success?
- How can we strengthen teacher and student work to support greater success?
- What scaffolds need to be put in place for students who have not mastered prerequisite skills?
- What enrichment augmentations can support deeper learning for students who demonstrate early success?
- How can we make evident our shifts in beliefs and aspirations?

The team will work together on the answers as it strengthens the lesson. It may find it needs some additional expert assistance with this task.

Tool 5.5 may be helpful for recording your learning agenda.

Rehearse enhanced lessons

Rehearsing lessons gives the team the critical opportunity to practice the new knowledge and skills we gained through our learning. In addition, practicing in front of peers may accomplish two important outcomes. The "teachers" strengthens expertise and the "students" comprehend more fully the learning

that they will be asking of their students. It has been previously cited that this is a key tenet of effective professional learning. These questions may be helpful at this point:

- Which lessons or lesson segments would benefit from rehearsal?
- Which learning team member will serve as teacher with others serving as students?
- Would it be helpful to have different members focus on different aspects of the lesson?
- How do we engage as students at the same time we take notes for refinement?

Tool 5.5 may be helpful for recording your learning agenda.

Refine lessons

As soon as possible after the team has completed its practice sessions, members should take time to discuss observations and determine how to refine the lesson(s). As noted earlier, it will be most helpful if the team schedules these two tasks in the same time period. During the refinement step the team may benefit from considering the following questions:

- What seemed to work well? Where were we challenged?
- Did the lesson proceed as we envisioned?
- Are there any corrections or modifications we want to make before taking it to the classroom?
- Are we feeling confident and do we have any evidence that it will lead to our desired outcomes for our students?

Tool 5.5 may be helpful for recording your learning agenda.

4. Schedule and engage in learning

There are always more things the team will want to learn and practice than the schedule will allow.

A case study: Focused learning

Jane's team has spent the last three weeks digging deeply into one of their new state standards focused on using academic language. They reviewed seminal as well as emerging research. They studied a variety of websites that offered specific suggestions for integrating academic language into their regular routines. They examined some of their past lessons to see where they had missed potential opportunities for reinforcing academic vocabulary. They ultimately developed a modified Innovation Configuration map to guide the implementation of new practices they want to integrate more regularly into their classrooms. After they completed this task they identified the intended outcomes and the formative assessments they would use to measure student progress. Then they focused on the lessons they had scheduled for the next three weeks and looked for particular opportunities to increase their focus on academic vocabulary. Each team member took one lesson and presented it to rest of the team so they could collectively refine it for individual use. After they concluded their learning agenda, the team looked forward to implementing the refined lessons in the classroom and checking the results.

Fortunately, the learning cycle is a continuous improvement process that signals that learning does not end at the conclusion of a particular cycle. Rather team members will know that their work can be revisited the next time similar issues are raised in discussions as well as the following year when they revisit this section of the curriculum.

More urgent are the important decisions teams will need to make to ensure they are prepared to begin the unit according to their schedule. Mapping backwards from that date and filling in the critical learning exercises will help the team to complete its learning agenda. The team can use Tool 5.5 to help complete its schedule.

Once the learning agenda is launched, team members expect that everyone is keeping commitments, supporting one another, and applying pressure among themselves, as needed, so that everyone stays on track. During this time team members are learning individually and collaboratively through a carefully planned progression of experiences designed for specific results. They are connecting their learning to their goals and collaborating with their colleagues to assess their progress. They are taking time for practice and reflection to determine how the process and content of their learning is influencing their practices and beliefs. Soon, learning reaches the implementation stage, which is covered fully in the next chapter. Student work and performance will tell the team whether their goals and learning choices were good ones.

References

Australian Institute for Teaching and School Leadership (AITSL). (2014). *Designing professional learning.* Available at www.aitsl.edu.au/docs/default-source/default-document-library/designing_professional_learning_report.pdf?sfvrsn=4

Calvert, L. (2016). *Moving from compliance to agency: What teachers need to make professional learning work.* Oxford, OH: Learning Forward & NCTAF.

Carnegie Mellon University. (2015a). Align assessments with objectives. In online chapter, *Whys and hows of assessment: Assessment basics.* [Website]. Available at www.cmu.edu/teaching/assessment/howto/basics/objectives.html

Carnegie Mellon University. (2015b). Why should assessments, learning objectives, and instructional strategies be aligned? In online chapter, *Whys and hows of assessment: Assessment basics.* [Website]. Available at www.cmu.edu/teaching/assessment/basics/alignment.html

Desimone, L.M., Porter, A.C., Garet, M.S., Yoon, K.S., Birman, B.F. (2002). Effect of professional development on teachers' instruction: Results from a three-year longitudinal study. *Education Evaluation and Policy Analysis, 24*(2), 81–112.

Goddard, Y. L., Goddard, R. D., & Tschannen-Moran, M. (2007). *Theoretical and empirical investigation of teacher collaboration for school improvement and student achievement in public elementary schools. Teachers College Record, 109*(4), 877–896.

Hargreaves, A. & Fullan, M. (2012). *Professional capital: Transforming teaching in every school.* New York, NY: Teachers College Press.

Hattie, J. (2009). *Visible learning: A synthesis of over 800 meta-analyses relating to achievement.* New York, NY: Taylor & Francis Group.

Hirsh, S., Psencik, M., & Brown, F. (2014). *Becoming a learning system.* Oxford, OH: Learning Forward.

Jensen, B., Sonnemann, J., Roberts-Hull, K. & Hunter, A. (2016). *Beyond PD: Teacher Professional Learning in High-Performing Systems.* Washington, DC: National Center on Education and the Economy.

Joyce, B. & Showers, B. (2002). *Designing training and peer coaching: Our needs for learning.* Alexandria, VA: ASCD.

Knowles, M. (1973). *The adult learner.* Houston, TX: Gulf Publishing Company.

Learning Forward. (2011). *Standards for Professional Learning.* Oxford, OH: Author.

Reflections

- We can describe the relationship between the Learning Forward Learning Designs standard and this phase of the learning cycle.

- We understand, respect, and apply principles of adult learning when choosing learning designs to address our learning goals.

- We understand appropriate uses of various learning strategies and know when to apply each.

- We can develop a learning agenda that leads to the intended educator and student learning outcomes.

- We have a reasonable framework to guide the attainment of student and educator learning goals.

Mezirow, J. (1997). Transformative learning: Theory to practice. In P. Cranton (Ed.), Transformative learning in action: Insights from practice. *New directions for adult and continuing education, No. 74* (pp. 5–12). San Francisco, CA: Jossey-Bass.

Roy, P. (2013). *School-based professional learning for implementing the common core. Unit 3: Learning designs.* Oxford, OH: Learning Forward. Available at https://learningforward.org/publications/implementing-common-core/professional-learning-units

Timperley, H., Wilson, A., Barrar, H., & Fung, I. (2007). *Teacher professional learning and development: Best Evidence Synthesis Iteration.* Wellington: Ministry of Education.

Vella, J. (2002). *Learning to listen, learning to teach.* Montpelier, VT: Global Learning Partners, Inc.

Tools index for chapter 5

Tool	Title	Use
5.1	Studying learning theories for students	Use this tool to examine Universal Design for Learning research and resources and implications for learning and lesson design.
5.2	Understanding principles of adult learning	Use this tool to review and reflect on principles of adult learning and their application to this stage of the learning cycle.
5.3	Reviewing summary of evidence on effective professional learning	Use this resource if you are reviewing research literature on effective professional learning or seeking rationale for team learning.
5.4	Examining learning designs	Use this tool to extend knowledge of various learning designs and as a reference for future planning.
5.5	Designing a learning agenda	Use this tool to consider the action planning template you will use guide your work together through Stages 3–5.

CHAPTER 6

Implement new learning

Where are we now?

We regularly improve our practice as a result of our learning.

STRONGLY AGREE   AGREE   NO OPINION   DISAGREE   STRONGLY DISAGREE

We apply the Implementation standard in transferring our new learning to our practice.

STRONGLY AGREE   AGREE   NO OPINION   DISAGREE   STRONGLY DISAGREE

We have many options for accessing support and feedback as we implement new learning in our classrooms.

STRONGLY AGREE   AGREE   NO OPINION   DISAGREE   STRONGLY DISAGREE

We use multiple sources of feedback to guide our implementation improvement efforts.

STRONGLY AGREE   AGREE   NO OPINION   DISAGREE   STRONGLY DISAGREE

We conduct discussions among team members regarding implementation challenges associated with new practices, lessons, etc., as a regular source of support for our work.

STRONGLY AGREE   AGREE   NO OPINION   DISAGREE   STRONGLY DISAGREE

Overview

In Chapter 6 the discussion turns to the implementation stage during which teams apply new learning with students. Team members may turn again to Tool 2.2: Reviewing the Learning Cycle to check their progress on developing a plan for making sure they have necessary resources, access to feedback, and job-embedded support for implementing new strategies and supporting adaptation as necessary.

The chapter covers the recursive nature of implementation and describes tools that teams may use to support and assess their progress through the stage (see also Tool 5.5: Designing a Learning Agenda). The discussion ends with action steps that a team may take to support successful application. Finally, the steps also help team members telescope from tending to the details of a newly implemented lesson to minding the big picture of progression through the stage. Some of those big-picture issues include informing administrators of progress and making requests for support, as appropriate, from school leadership to create or strengthen the conditions needed for successful implementation.

Why does implementation matter?

At this stage in the learning cycle, team members are shifting from their trials to actual use. They have refined their units and lessons based on their new learning. Although they may have developed confidence in their lessons, they realize that everything may go differently than planned. As a result, before they teach a planned and rehearsed lesson, team members also arrange for support and feedback to assist them with that work. Recognizing that support and feedback can come in many forms, they choose a form

(e.g. coaching, co-teaching, or observation) that may be most desirable given the complexity and extent of the change they are attempting to make. During the learning stage, teams have had multiple opportunities to practice with their peers, but the true test of new learning is when team members transfer it into the classroom and observe its impact on students. Then, they get to see whether their practice accelerates progress toward intended student outcomes. Before they get to this point, learning teams will have moved through the complex stage of practicing, learning, and applying new learning. They may be more likely to see success if they take actions grounded in change research and implementation science.

Invest in implementation for results

Research on the impact of quality implementation of programs and services has shown that without a focus on implementation of practice, outcomes may not be achieved as expected; in some cases a poorly implemented program may produce harmful results (Fixsen, Naoom, Blase, Friedman, & Wallace, 2005; Hall & Hord, 2015). Most of the failures attributed to professional development are the result of poor implementation. Specifically, say Dean Fixsen and colleagues (2005), failure may be due to the lack of attention on the complex processes of implementation, or "delineating and testing scale-up processes" (p. 2). People often are motivated and committed at the beginning of any new change initiative, but when faced with competing priorities and new obstacles to overcome, they find themselves backing away from their commitments to the implementation phase of change. It's not uncommon to hear something like the following: "I am glad to study these strategies with you, but don't ask me to use them in my classroom just when I have everything finally going the way I want it."

In that example, then, studying research, best practices, or even practicing new strategies is a waste of time and effort without an equivalent understanding and commitment to put new learning into practice. Professional development pioneers Michael Fullan and the late Susan Loucks-Horsley had a particular way of describing how each interviewed potential clients. Whoever was interviewing would draw a long line across a chalkboard using it as an indicator of the time it would take to successfully institutionalize a new program into a school system. Then he or she would draw a line down the middle and say to the decision makers, "To the right of the line is where the hard work begins —it represents the implementation phase, and if you are not committed to the resources required to see this through, then I am not interested in working with you." (see Tool 6.1: Digging Deeper into Design and Implementation for additional resources for implementation).

The linkage between high-quality curriculum, research-based practices, and support is critical to outcomes. In the vignette on page 82, read how a master teacher in a Texas school provided coaching and modeling as a 3rd-grade teacher team practiced and applied a new literacy strategy.

The Standards for Professional Learning (2011) devote a standard to implementation:

> Implementation: Professional learning that increases educator effectiveness and results for all students applies research on change and sustains support for implementation of professional learning for long-term change. (Learning Forward, p. 44)

Some of the more critical elements of effective implementation are referenced in it, namely, the application of findings from research on change process to support long-term change in practice; the integration of a variety of supports for individuals, teams, and schools; and the integration of feedback and reflection to support continuous improvement in practice (Learning Forward, 2011, p. 44).

Decades of research on the change process provide guidance on how educators may transition from early stages of managing change to focusing on the impact it is having on their students. A number of change models and diagnostic tools exist that can be applied to support individuals, teams, and schools as they work through this stage.

Recognize that change is hard

Everyone knows that change is hard. The first steps team members take to implement new knowledge and skills often fail to go as planned or immediately lead to intended outcomes. Even though a team has been careful in preparing for the change, any member also knows what can happen in a classroom when a unit, lesson plan, or strategy goes array. Chaos may quickly break out, and the teacher may find her confidence eroding to attempt any further changes. Change, after all, takes time.

So, teams take a critical action step forward when they acknowledge the difficulty of this stage of the work. Equally important are the peer pressure and support associated with the shared commitment to take this next step. Celebrating small victories as well as big battles will play a key role in sustaining the effort required for making substantive changes.

Understand implementation science

Implementation science has been a field of study in several disciplines since the 1970s. For much of that time, education researchers, often with government sponsorship, have conducted basic and evaluation research on the implementation of an innovative program to improve practice in schools. Some early models of the relationship between federally funded dissemination efforts and local education practice show giver-recipient relationships in which teachers were "pressured into action" to participate in implementation of school improvement initiative (Grimmett, 1987, p. 6). Other large-scale studies of the change process and improvement in local schools documented a complex network of actors including teachers, administrators, students, and change agents interacting to apply education research findings in a process of change (Berman & McLaughlin, 1978; Hall, 1978; Huberman & Crandall, 1983). Efforts to develop more active relationships between implementation researchers and education practitioners have spanned the past four decades. The last decade has seen growth in the expectation that educators will directly use and even participate in implementation research in order to improve practice and, ultimately, student outcomes. Direct engagement of local educators in education research also improves the relevance and rigor of research, thereby also improving the process of applying those findings in schools (Fixsen, et al., 2009; GAO, 2013). Karen Blase and colleagues (2015) highlight the relationship between evidence-based implementation strategies and improved education:

> Purposeful attention to implementation requires using *evidence-based and evidence-informed implementation strategies and frameworks* to improve teachers' and administrators' confidence and competence, to create hospitable organizations and system environments for new ways of work…In short, attention to implementation science acknowledges that improved education will require attention to two outcomes: implementation outcomes and intervention [student] outcomes. Implementation outcomes focus on changes

in teacher and staff behaviors … in order to support better ways of educating students. Student outcomes…must be preceded by implementation outcomes; students cannot benefit from the evidence-based instruction they do not receive. (p. 4)

Recent federal legislation, *Every Student Succeeds Act* (P.L. 114–95), makes that relationship explicit with language that calls for greater consideration and application of evidence-based findings.

Implementation science elevates the importance of focused attention on application of new practices. Without it, teams may feel they are on their own when they complete the learning agenda. Each person continues to function as an independent contractor with full autonomy over what gets transferred into the classroom. As a result of implementation science and the learning team cycle, team members move collectively beyond learning into action. In this stage, the team delineates what will happen in classrooms with team members and students for the next six weeks or for whatever period of time it is organized to support. The learning team cycle details all the critical steps for identifying, applying, and assessing evidence-based practices.

How do teams progress through this stage?

Prepare for the implementation dip

Over the years, educators have become familiar with the phrase, implementation dip. They know to expect that behaviors, outcomes, test scores may get worse before they get better. It is one thing to philosophically accept and understand that possibility and another to experience and justify when it happens. Team members may experience the implementation

Figure 6.1: Seven Stages of Concern

The Concerns-Based Adoption Model outlines seven Stages of Concern that offer a way to understand and then address educators' common concerns about change.

Stage 6: Refocusing

Begins refining the innovation to improve student learning results.

❑ "I have some ideas about something that would work even better than this."

Stage 5: Collaboration

Interested in working with colleagues to make the change effective.

❑ "I'm concerned about relating what I'm doing to what other instructors are doing."

❑ "I want to see more cooperation among teachers as we work with this innovation."

Stage 4: Consequence

Interested in the impact on students or the school.

❑ "How is using this going to affect students?"

❑ "I'm concerned about whether I can change this in order to ensure that students will learn better as a result of introducing this idea."

Stage 3: Management

Concerned about how the change will be managed in practice.

❑ "I seem to be spending all of my time getting materials ready."

❑ "I'm concerned that we'll be spending more time in meetings."

❑ "Where will I find the time to plan my lessons or take care of the record keeping required to do this well?"

Stage 2: Personal

Wants to know the personal impact of the change.

❑ "How is this going to affect me?"

❑ "I'm concerned about whether I can do this."

❑ "How much control will I have over the way I use this?"

Stage 1: Informational

Interested in some information about the change.

❑ "I want to know more about this innovation."

❑ "There is a lot I don't know about this but I'm reading and asking questions."

Stage 0: Awareness

Aware that an innovation is being introduced but not really interested or concerned with it.

❑ "I am not concerned about this innovation."

❑ "I don't really know what this innovation involves."

Source: *Taking Charge of Change,* by Shirley Hord, William Rutherford, Leslie Huling-Austin, and Gene Hall. Copyright 1987 SEDL. Reprinted with permission.

dip during their early stages of trying new practices; with pressure for constant improvement, the dip explanation doesn't always suffice and they may need to plan to minimize the effect. Michael Fullan (2001) writes that

> All successful schools experience implementation dips as they move forward. The implementation dip is literally a dip in performance and confidence as one encounters an innovation that requires new skills and new understandings. (p. 41)

Team members can support one another through the dip by taking time to listen to one another's concerns and identify the worst of their fears. Perhaps they could consider responses should any trepidations become reality. Peers may also offer individual team members additional opportunities for practice to help increase overall confidence. Team members may decide that co-implementation in the beginning will be the most valuable support they can provide. What teachers need and appreciate most is help that will reduce perception of the dip and accelerate improvement of student understanding and performance.

Apply change research tools

Up to this point, the discussion of implementation has considered why change is challenging and why support is critical. When educators put what they have learned into practice, change will happen. At times, teachers will take substantive new actions to make changes; often, they can easily integrate new practices into their normal routines. With models such as the Concerns-Based Adoption Model (CBAM), change

Figure 6.2: The Levels of Use of an innovation

Levels of use	Typical behaviors
VI. Renewal	The user is seeking more effective alternatives to the established use of the innovation.
V. Integration	The user is making deliberate efforts to coordinate with others in using the innovation.
VIB. Refinement	The user is making changes to increase outcomes.
IVA. Routine	The user is making few or no changes and has an established pattern of use.
III. Mechanical	The user is making changes to better organize use of the innovation.
II. Preparation	The user has definite plans to begin using the innovation.
I. Orientation	The user is taking the initiative to learn more about the innovation.
0. Non-Use	The user has no interest, is taking no action.

Source: *Taking Charge of Change,* by Shirley Hord, William Rutherford, Leslie Huling-Austin, and Gene Hall. Copyright 1987 SEDL. Reprinted with permission.

research provides a foundation as well as guidance for responding to the predictable challenges of the change process. The CBAM contains three key diagnostic dimensions, each with tools that change agents have used to support their improvement efforts and that team members may use: Stages of Concern process, Levels of Use interview guide, and Innovation Configuration map (Hall & Hord, 2015).

Stages of Concern

The Stages of Concern diagnostic tool lets team members know how an individual responds to and manages change. It can apply to any sort of change, including change in one's personal or professional life. The seven stages describe the reactions, attitudes, and concerns of an individual at each stage (see Figure 6.1).

By identifying the precise concern, team members and others have better information to guide how they help their colleagues address such concerns. Based on the insights gathered from the questionnaires team members can create or identify *interventions* that may assist their colleagues or in some cases the entire team to address the concern (see Tool 6.2: Recognizing and Responding to Colleagues' Concerns for an instrument they may use during this stage). As team members progress through the changes the questions shift from personal and management to substantive impact questions. Ultimately, the goal is to help everyone move through to the highest levels of concerns.

Levels of Use

The Levels of Use interview guide (see Figure 6.2) is an additional resource that teams may use during this stage, particularly when they are trying to implement a complex unit or lesson. The interview tool helps teams determine at what level they or other team members are using, both individually and collectively, the designated lessons or unit. Levels of Use range

from nonuse to renewal (see Tool 6.3: Understanding the Levels of Use Diagnostic Tool to use the interview guide during this stage). A team can use the tool to measure and report on its progress toward full implementation. Team members also may use this tool as part of their monitoring plan (Hall & Hord, 2015).

Innovation Configuration

Another powerful tool is an Innovation Configuration (IC) map. The map is a rubric-like instrument that teams may use to paint a clear picture of what high-quality implementation looks like. The team may work together to create an Innovation Configuration map that they can then use to guide and focus their efforts (Hall & Hord, 2015). Similar to the Levels of Use Interview Scale, the IC maps can also be used during the monitoring and assessment stage that follows.

When teams commit to developing IC maps they detail the precise actions they expect to see taken by the key persons responsible for implementing a desired program or strategy. The IC maps are typically written to define behaviors that range from basic to proficient levels of implementation. In some cases IC maps are made available for teams to study so they can better understand the practices they will be expected to apply. On the other hand learning team members experience powerful learning when they write their own IC map because the process produces a deep, shared understanding of the practices they will apply. The conversations that occur during the development of a map result in a common language, shared vision, and profound understanding and appreciation of the journey the team commits to together (Hall & Hord, 2015).

Figure 6.3 shows an excerpt from an IC map of the Implementation standard for teachers. Teams will be able to assess the quality of their implementation plans using this IC map.

Figure 6.3: Innovation Configuration map of the Implementation standard for teachers

6.1 Apply change research					
Level 1	Level 2	Level 3	Level 4	Level 5	Level 6
Desired outcome 6.1.1: Develops capacity to apply research on change to support implementation of professional learning.					
• Reviews, with colleagues, research studies and examples of exemplary change practices (IC maps, SoC, LoU, RPLIM, PDSA, etc.) to develop own understanding of and skills needed to facilitate the change process. • Participates in additional professional learning about the change process to address opportunities and problems of practice. • Develops and applied, with principal and colleagues, knowledge and skills needed to participate in the change process.	• Reviews, with colleagues, research studies and examples of exemplary change practices (IC maps, SoC, LoU, RPLIM, PDSA, etc.) to develop own understanding of and skills needed to facilitate the change process. • Participates in additional professional learning about the change process to address opportunities and problems of practice. • Discusses, with colleagues, information to increase understanding of the change process.	• Reviews research studies and examples of exemplary practice (IC maps, SoC, LoU, RPLIM, PDSA, etc.) to develop own understanding of and skills needed to facilitate the change process. • Participates in additional professional learning about the change process to address opportunities and problems of practice.	• Reads articles, papers, and reports about the change process.	• Fails to engage in ongoing professional learning about the change process.	

Source: *Standards into practice: School-based roles. Innovation Configuration maps for Standards for Professional Learning,* page 77. Copyright 2012 Learning Forward.

Seek and sustain support

Sustaining support for implementation is another key aspect of the Implementation standard. Although major program changes require continued support for three to five years (Fullan, 2001), learning teams have the benefit of the iterative cycle of learning to improve their practices over time. To achieve their immediate goals, teams need job-embedded support such as that available from coaches or peers to help them apply their learning during this stage. For learning team members, others sources of such support may include the following:

- Observing a colleague. Some team members, though feeling very prepared, may still want to watch the new practices applied one more time. Watching the students' reactions may instill the confidence they seek to do it on their own.

- Co-teaching with a peer. It can be helpful to try a new strategy or introduce an improved lesson with a colleague. This can allow for one person to focus on the reaction of students and the other to focus on the strategy.

- Inviting a coach to help. The coach may be in the classroom to make notes on implementation or step in if help is deemed necessary.

- Accessing a just-in-time coach who observes from a distance. This emerging option arises from use of broad- or narrowcast technologies; moreover, because the teacher is broadcasting a lesson, the coach or mentor is able to provide immediate support through an ear bud or other communications device.

In general, successful implementation requires effective support that is available when the team member needs it most and is part of a continuous process of improvement.

Seek and exchange feedback

Availability of constructive feedback is another key component of successful implementation. Feedback has a variety of meanings and can also be influenced by the context in which it is delivered. For the purpose of the cycle of learning, team members look for data and listen for perspectives on the quality of their practice and what they can do to improve. Given that interest, there are a variety of sources that support growth and improvement.

Feedback should come from multiple sources and in multiple forms. Facilitators, coaches, colleagues, supervisors, and students can provide valuable feedback. Eleanor Drago-Severson (2011) says that specific and precise feedback given during the learning process supports learners. Learners will make small corrections and build greater strength and competence when peers, coaches, and principals give them regular, precise feedback about what they are doing well. Team leaders and colleagues offer valuable sources of feedback, particularly if there are predetermined areas of focus for the observation. This is one case when IC maps are valuable, because if the team has clarity about how the practice should occur and the desired student response, the IC map can guide the kind of feedback that will be most helpful to the colleague. Coaches and supervisors can also provide feedback and have the additional advantage of considering the practices in light of individual, team, and schoolwide goals. External content experts offer valuable feedback because they often not only understand the process but also have the content knowledge to give specific feedback in both areas. There have been cases when a teacher's poor content expertise was masked by strong student engagement and observers did not recognize the problem. As a result, it is valuable to ensure that there is always a feedback loop from the content experts.

Teachers apply proven reading strategy with modeling and support

For two years, I taught in a Dallas-area elementary school serving more than 700 students, most of whom qualified for free-and-reduced lunch. When I joined as a master teacher in the Teacher Advancement Program (TAP), I coached the 3rd-grade team of six teachers. Across that grade level students were struggling in many different areas. But the school's main focus for the year was to improve reading scores in all grade levels from a 22% to 80% passing rate on the reading state assessment.

Equipped with that knowledge — and specific data about 3rd-grade reading needs — I started the Implementation cycle weeks before the team met as I researched strategies that the teachers would learn. After choosing a strategy, I field tested it with a sample of students from all 3rd- grade classrooms. I used this test to modify the strategy to meet our students' needs and determine the best way to "chunk" the strategy when teaching it during our professional learning sessions. The strategy became known as the KIS Strategy, or KEYWORDS, INFERENCE, and SUPPORT with background knowledge.

During our first weekly professional development meeting, known as "cluster," the teachers analyzed the data and came to the same conclusion that I had: The biggest need for our 3rd graders in reading was making inferences and drawing conclusions. We developed the following cycle goal:

By the end of the cycle, students will increase their ability to draw conclusions about the structures and elements of nonfiction and fiction text and provide evidence to support their understanding as measured by a pre- and postassessment. Students will increase their scores by 25%.

For several reasons teachers felt confident about this goal: It was a short time period, it was specific in what area students would improve, and it was realistic with the 25% increase in measured performance. Now that we had set the goal, we were ready to work.

To make the most of limited implementation and reflection time, we followed the same protocol each

Richardson Independent School District	
Founded	1854
Campuses	55
Student enrollment	38,600
Neighborhood	Northern Dallas County
Demographics:	
Asian	6.9%
Black	21.6%
Hispanic	40.0%
White	28.3%
Free or Reduced-Priced Lunch	57.3%
English Language Learners	25.5%
Special Education	10.3%
Attendance	96.5%

week for eight weeks: First, we would identify the need for the meeting and I would model the new "chunk" of the KIS strategy. While modeling, I would "step out" of my role as teacher and ask team members to reflect on what they were seeing me do or ask clarifying questions. Then, teachers would take time to develop their skills. Sometimes they practiced how they would teach the strategy during the next week. The next step in the protocol was "Apply," which occurred during the following week when teachers applied the new learning with their students. About halfway into the cycle, one teacher felt the strategy wasn't clicking for her students. I observed her and the students to gather more information. During our next cluster she brought in student work showing that students were struggling with the inference part of the strategy, and shared why she thought that was happening. As a team, we analyzed the work and suggested ways she might adapt her instruction. We also developed guiding questions she could use when she saw students moving in the wrong direction. Throughout the cycle, all teachers collected student artifacts so we could evaluate the impact of each lesson, then we identified the need for the next cluster meeting.

After eight weeks I gave teachers a postassessment to administer to all of the 3rd graders. During our final cluster, we compared and analyzed the pre- and postassessment data; our students had increased passing rates by 22% — not quite reaching our goal, but close. We celebrated our students' progress at the final cluster of the cycle.

Leslie Ceballos, K–4 science instructional specialist
Dallas, Texas

Limitations in staff or time may challenge teams to secure the amount of feedback they most desire. Teams may find they can have varying feedback — in kind and degree — if they rethink the nature of feedback. By thinking of feedback as a learning process, team members give themselves access to a wider variety of sources and opportunities for requesting, receiving, and providing feedback (Killion, 2015). In addition, with technological advances teachers can record lessons and share them in a number of online platforms and gather feedback from a variety of sources.

The most important feedback source will be input from students. Student feedback tells teachers much about how successfully they have applied their learning. Such feedback is generally immediate and tied to the goals the team set earlier in the cycle. Of course, student performance on formative assessments will be most valuable in determining whether the strategy, lesson, or unit delivered on its intended expectations. But, watching for indications of student engagement or struggle also will help educators know whether their learning agenda followed the best path. For example, in independent reading sessions teachers could sense when students lose interest in reading by noticing how rapidly they turn pages or how they attempt to distract other students around them.

Finally, during this stage feedback should be a daily occurrence that informs the ongoing team debriefing sessions. As teams identify challenges, members will solve problems, brainstorm, and support one other. They will bring in student work to calibrate their expectations and to determine whether they are on the right path to their goals. This is the ultimate source of feedback that helps to sustain progress through the challenges of change (see Tool 6.4: Giving and Receiving Feedback for help developing team members' skills giving and receiving feedback).

Identify barriers and strategies for addressing them

When teams commit to continuous improvement processes they likely expect to face and overcome challenges. But beyond acknowledging that likelihood, few take time to build into their routines how they will handle and overcome any difficulties. Because the learning cycle is an iterative process, no one can predict and then remove all the challenges that may surface. Consequently, the team should expect that unanticipated challenges and barriers will surface at any time. Teams should expect to use some of their time together to identify and discuss barriers and apply protocols or consult others for help in resolving them.

Identify opportunities related to policies, resources, and technology

During implementation, teams may recognize opportunities to improve conditions to support and sustain new practices. Teams can build support for the team learning cycle by scheduling time with administrators to share observations and recommendations about potential changes to policies that could be more supportive of the changes they are putting in place. They might identify resources or technology needed to sustain changes or support small groups of teachers or students who need extra assistance to achieve team goals. Central office leaders and administrators are better positioned to support such requests when teams keep them informed in throughout the cycle and have authentic stories about practice and evidence of results to back up their requests.

LEARNING GOAL EXAMPLE	Problem solving for 6th graders
Revisiting the example team of 6th-grade teachers (see p. 50) shows that after they complete their learning agendas in Stage 3 and determine how they are modifying instruction or adapting or refining their lessons, they plan for transferring their learning into the classroom. During Stage 4, they must schedule any lessons they intend to teach based on what they've learned and at the same time identify the various forms of support they each want or need to support their practice. An example of a plan may include the following:	Supported application. During a six-week period, team members work together to implement and assess lessons they studied in Stage 3. **Week 1:** Teachers co-teach the first week's lesson then meet to discuss. **Week 2:** They teach the second lesson independently and reflect independently. **Week 3:** They teach the third lesson with an observer, then meet for feedback from an observer. **Weeks 4–5:** They teach the fourth and fifth lessons and videotape themselves; they reflect and then bring student work for team discussion. **Week 6:** They teach the final lesson. The team members reflect individually and then meet as a team to make final assessment on the implementation of the learning from the earlier stage.

Taking action

1. Develop plan for implementing units and lessons

A key purpose of a learning agenda is the transformation of practice to achieve better outcomes for students. Team members introduce these practices in units and lessons. Then, members measure the lesson's impact on student learning through formative and summative assessments. In the process, teams make an important transition: They evolve from acquiring new learning and developing new skills and practices to determining where those new practices best fit in the overall instructional plan.

At this point in the learning cycle, the learning team is excited about applying new learning in the classroom. As with any planning process, team members will set aside time exclusively to plan for transfer of learning to the classroom. They will consider when and how their lessons, strategies, and assessments will be implemented and when and how they will access the job-embedded support they need for success. While the school schedule may provide the framework for sequencing the work, the team must add precise details of their action planning. Filling in the schedule is detail oriented, and some members of the team may be more skillful than others at this aspect of the work. Once scheduling is completed everyone will be on the same page of the plan and ready to continue the application of their learning.

2. Use tools or resources to guide implementation and support adaptation as necessary

During this stage, team members identify

resources available to support classroom-based implementation. They consider the strengths, weaknesses, and appropriateness of each for this set of goals. Their decisions will be affected by the context in which they work together. Among the many resources they may have at their disposal are schedules that are flexible enough to permit co-teaching, peer observation, and instructional walk-throughs. Members of a learning team may find ways to support their self-reflection with technology-enhanced tools. For example, team members in some sites may use classroom-based video capture or have access to remote coaching.

During the learning stage, individuals and teams may have identified and/or developed different tools or resources to assist with the implementation stage. These tools may include Innovation Configuration maps to support individual planning and reflection or coaching and feedback sessions.

The team may have created other rubrics to use to assess student work. The rubrics may be shared with students so they understand the criteria by which they will be assessed. The rubrics also provide teachers with important reminders of the outcomes they are seeking for their students.

3. Enlist job-embedded support

Job-embedded support typically references the support educators receive from peers, coaches, administrators, and technical assistance providers before, during, or after classroom instruction. The opportunities themselves may vary in format, but all job-embedded learning is always centered on issues of actual practice and takes place in the school (see Tool 6.5: Identifying and Prioritizing Sources of Support). Teachers may experience job-embedded learning alone or with a coach. For example, on his own shortly before or after instruction and away from students, a teacher may analyze the

work of two students and write about it for his portfolio (Croft, et al., 2010, p. 3). In another instance, a teacher may confer with his mentor during planning for and after presenting a lesson. After observing that lesson, the mentor describes strengths and weaknesses in the teacher's instructional planning and implementation. Her support prompts him to incorporate changes in his instruction the following day (Croft, et al., 2010, p. 3).

The most appropriate type of job-embedded support depends on the learner's goal, stage of concern, level of expertise, or personal preference. The schedule should take into consideration the various forms of support requested by team members to facilitate successful implementation. While most support is scheduled, there is always the chance that administrator or supervisor walk-throughs or observations occur offering another type of support and feedback.

4. Engage in feedback process with evidence from others to inform continuous improvement

The team will identify other data to guide implementation as well as contribute to the assessment and monitoring phase that comes up next. This feedback may surface from a variety of sources: It may be part of the follow up to team members' various observation and coaching visits scheduled in the implementation plan. Or team members may identify specific data that they want to use to guide daily improvements and assess the overall learning and application. They may gather student data through technological devices as well as from authentic classroom work or assessments. They may also decide to collect student data that address academic and behavioral concerns.

During this stage, team members may validate their perceptions by asking colleagues, coaches, and supervisors to observe and provide feedback. Each

Reflections

- We have confidence in our plans to implement our new learning, programs, and innovations.

- We have a deep appreciation for the complexity of the change process and feel confident in using tools and resources to assist our efforts.

- We see the value of and intend to use IC maps to assist us in achieving fidelity of implementation of our new strategies, programs, and innovations.

- We have many options for accessing immediate and longer term support and know how to use each.

- We value feedback from multiple sources and are deliberate in how we use it to strengthen practice.

member may bring to team meetings evidence related to indicators of performance and ask colleagues for feedback and support. Such discussions tied to authentic classroom artifacts can promote even deeper understanding and crystalize the commitment to sustaining the practices over time.

Ultimately student feedback is most meaningful when it is directly linked to short and long-term student learning goals. Student feedback can be gathered during or at the end of classes. During classes, teachers can identify and gather data on those behaviors they seek to impact. Student work provides feedback on levels of learning. At the end of class, teachers can gather attitude, understanding, and application data from their students. Student surveys provide information to the teacher on a variety of indicators that can inform instruction and improve outcomes for students. When teachers examine student work together they receive feedback on their instruction and strengthen their understanding of which students need more attention to be successful in achieving the learning goals.

References

Blase, K. A., Fixsen, D. L., Sims, B.J., & Ward, C.S. (2015). *Implementation science: Changing hearts, minds, behavior, and systems to improve educational outcomes.* Paper presented at the Wing Institute's Ninth Annual Summit on Evidence-Based Education, Berkeley, CA. Available at https://www.researchgate.net/publication/279529943_Implementation_Science_Changing_Hearts_Minds_Behavior_and_Systems_to_Improve_Educational_Outcomes

Berman, P. & McLaughlin, M.W. (1978). *Federal programs supporting educational change, Vol. VIII: Implementing and sustaining innovations.* Santa Monica, CA: Rand Corporation.

Croft, A., Coggeshall, J., Dolan, M., Powers, E. (with Killion, J.). (2010). *Job-embedded professional development: What it is, who is responsible, and how to get it done well. Issue brief.* Washington, DC: National Comprehensive Center for Teacher Quality.

Drago-Severson, E. (2011, October). How adults learn forms the foundation of the Learning Designs standard. *JSD, 32*(5), 10–12.

Every Student Succeeds Act of 2015, P.L. 114–95 §§ 1–9215. Available at https://www.gpo.gov/fdsys/pkg/PLAW-114publ95/pdf/PLAW-114publ95.pdf

Fixsen, D.L., Blase, K.A., Naoom, S.F., & Wallace, F. (2009). Core implementation components. (2009). *Research on Social Work Practice, 19*(5), 531–540. Available at http://rsw.sagepub.com/content/19/5/531

Fixsen, D. L., Naoom, S. F., Blase, K. A., Friedman, R. M., & Wallace, F. (2005). *Implementation Research: A synthesis of the literature (FMHI #231).* Tampa, FL: University of South Florida, Louis de la Parte Florida Mental Health Institute, The National Implementation Research Network.

Fullan, M. (2001). *Leading in a culture of change.* San Francisco, CA: Jossey-Bass.

GAO (United States Government Accountability Office). (2013). *Education research: Further improvements needed to ensure relevance and assess dissemination efforts.* (GAO 14–8). Washington, DC: Author.

Grimmett, P. (1987). The role of district supervisors in the implementation of peer coaching. *Journal of Curriculum and Supervision, 3*(1), 3–28.

Hall, G.E. (1978). *Implications for planned dissemination, implementation, and evaluation revealed in the SRI/NDN Evaluation and Levels of Use of the Innovation studies.* (Procedures for adopting educational innovations project.) Austin, TX: Research and Development Center for Teacher Education. Paper presented at the American Educational Research Association Annual Meeting, Toronto, Canada, March 27–31, 1978.

Hall, G. E. & Hord, S. M. (2015). *Implementing change: Patterns, principles and potholes (4th ed.).* Upper Saddle River, NJ: Pearson.

Huberman, A. M. & Crandall, D.P. (1983). *Implications for action: A study of dissemination efforts supporting school improvement: Volume IX. People, Policies, and Practices: Examining the Chain of Social Improvement,* Volumes I–X. Andover, MA: The Network.

Hord, S., Rutherford, W., Huling-Austin, L., & Hall, G. (1987). *Taking charge of change.* Alexandria, VA: ASCD.

Killion, J. (2015). *The feedback process: Transforming feedback for professional learning.* Oxford, OH: Learning Forward.

Learning Forward. (2011). *Standards for Professional Learning.* Oxford, OH: Author.

Learning Forward. (2012). *Standards into practice: School-based roles. Innovation Configuration maps for Standards for Professional Learning.* Oxford, OH: Author.

Tools index for chapter 6

Tool	Title	Use
6.1	Digging deeper into design and implementation	Use this tool to build knowledge regarding key components of the design and implementation stages of the learning cycle.
6.2	Recognizing and responding to colleagues' concerns	Use this tool to increase understanding of the Stages of Concern diagnostic tool and teams can use it during the implementation stage.
6.3	Understanding the Levels of Use diagnostic tool	Use this tool to increase understanding of Levels of Use and how teams can use it during implementation stage.
6.4	Giving and receiving feedback	Use this tool to support the development of feedback skills.
6.5	Identifying and prioritizing sources of support	Use this tool to plan for implementation support.

CHAPTER 7

Monitor, assess, and adjust practice

Where are we now?

We have processes in place to monitor, assess, and adjust the progress of our practice.

| STRONGLY AGREE | AGREE | NO OPINION | DISAGREE | STRONGLY DISAGREE |

We develop, access, and use tools and protocols for monitoring desired teacher and student actions.

| STRONGLY AGREE | AGREE | NO OPINION | DISAGREE | STRONGLY DISAGREE |

We have the autonomy, knowledge, and skills to appropriately adjust practice to achieve better outcomes.

| STRONGLY AGREE | AGREE | NO OPINION | DISAGREE | STRONGLY DISAGREE |

We develop, access, and use appropriate assessments for measuring and reporting impact.

| STRONGLY AGREE | AGREE | NO OPINION | DISAGREE | STRONGLY DISAGREE |

We regularly reflect to support deeper learning and make better decisions.

| STRONGLY AGREE | AGREE | NO OPINION | DISAGREE | STRONGLY DISAGREE |

Overview

In Chapter 7 discussions cover the importance of reflection on data that teams collect. This chapter also reviews various assessments and tools that learning teams may use to observe, monitor, and document the impact of their efforts thus far.

As they consider the data about students' responses to the team's instructional strategies, team members find that the tools they've used in earlier stages have recurring value. For this final stage, team members may also find it useful to glance over Tool 2.2: Reviewing the Learning Cycle or refer to Tool 5.5: Designing a Learning Agenda as they move through their shared reflection on outcomes to refine and determine next actions. Team members can use student work, assessment data, and observations to inform how they should adjust their practice to deepen students' understanding and improve behavioral and academic performance. By using assessments and other measurement tools regularly to collect data, teams can track the impact of their learning on student learning.

How does monitoring support ongoing improvement?

Once teachers take new practices into classrooms, they are excited to see how their new knowledge and skills will impact their students. As new professional learning is applied during the implementation stage, team members are gathering formal and informal data about what is working with their students and what isn't working. Their task is to use these data to refine their immediate implementation as well as inform future decisions.

Examine the team's learning cycle

In Stage 5: Monitor, assess, and adjust practice, teams ask questions such as, "What evidence do we have that shows we are making progress toward our goals?"; "What is the impact of our change on our practice and our students?"; "Where do we go from here?"; and "How can we apply what we are learning in this cycle to upcoming units or lessons?"

To answer those questions, team members draw insights from a variety of formal and informal sources, including classroom assessments and student work, as well as observations of students responding during class time. They refine their practices to improve student engagement, learning, and outcomes. Based on the student learning goals they've set, teams use their formative and summative assessments to measure precisely whether they have indeed accomplished what they planned to achieve. They use the results to guide necessary adjustments immediately as well as inform where they will focus next in the cycle of learning.

As teams monitor the outcome of their new classroom practices, they discover whether they are on the right path. By the end of this stage, the team will learn whether the decisions they made were the right ones for achieving the desired outcomes (see Figure 7.1). When they review the data, they may discover which actions seem to be on track and where they may need to revisit decisions or actions.

When they are in the monitoring stage of the learning cycle, teams collect and examine data to determine where they succeeded and what they still need to address. What they learn from their monitoring and assessment findings may lead team members to reexamine assumptions, choose new strategies, or strengthen their learning agenda to achieve the intended outcomes for this cycle.

Ideally, the results justify moving forward and launching a new cycle.

Check for behavior change

As discussed in Chapter 5, *being intentional about team learning* may be the one thing that distinguishes this learning cycle from others. In other cycles educators analyze data, diagnosis needs, set student goals, and put new plans into action. Because these plans are based on current levels of knowledge, they often include doubling down on old strategies rather than implementing new ones. Lacking new perspectives, new knowledge, or findings from current research, team members have few opportunities to recognize changes they may want to make.

For educators to improve their own practice, they must place as high a priority on their own learning as they do on student learning. For professional learning to be considered effective it must include both intentional learning and change in practice. However, intentional learning does not necessarily transfer to changed practice. The discussion of implementation in Chapter 6 shows the range of the support that educators may need to help them make the changes they desire. If they are truly committed to these changes, school leaders, teacher leaders, and team members will invest equally in implementation support and intentional learning.

During the monitoring stage of the cycle, both learning and implementation come under scrutiny. Team members look for evidence that they learned the content deeply so that they are able to apply it with students in a way that leads those students to grasp a concept and, ultimately, be more successful. If professional learning has been effective, the team members will have evidence that their practice is changing and

Figure 7.1: Review the learning cycle to assess progress and decisions

We will increase by 50% the 8th-grade Title I students who will:

Demonstrate proficiency and report increased efficacy in providing an objective summary of a text, including the theme and its relationship to the characters, setting, and plot.

By:

The end of six weeks.

If we learn:

How authors develop themes over the course of a literary text and what it takes for students to analyze how a theme is developed over the course of a text and produce an objective summary.

Using this means of professional learning:

- Studying the related curriculum lessons and units.
- Consulting with a coach and seeking online resources to fill gaps in understanding.
- Observing teachers who are successful with this population and outcome.

Applying our learning by:

Teaching modified lessons with a coach who observes and offers input.

And expecting more of our students to:

Demonstrate mastery by writing objective summaries of texts and effectively identifying themes and their relationships to characters, setting, and plot.

that their students are rising to the higher expectations and meeting the standards.

Reflect on practice

John Dewey is believed to have said, "We don't learn from experience. We learn from reflecting on experience." Accurate quotation notwithstanding, educators have long championed the value of reflection in professional learning. In his blog, "Edunators," Mark Clements (2016) muses that

> Reflection is an integral part of the learning process. … It requires educators to show humility and admit they can improve. We must be willing to practice reflection ourselves and model for our students so they may also learn the power of reflecting on their mistakes. (para. 13)

Reflection is a powerful component of the professional learning process and we include it in Stage 3 as well. A learner can use her reflections to motivate her to act and change her practice to improve student learning (York-Barr, Sommer, Ghere, & Montie, 2005). Teams may use Tool 7.1: Learning to Practice Reflection to facilitate their use of reflection processes to examine their experiences in a systematic way. Regular use of reflection can strengthen team member awareness throughout the learning cycle and help team members develop the discipline of reflective practice. Integrating reflective practice into the monitoring stage helps the team ensure that members do not jump to conclusions or judgments too quickly and, instead, arrive at recommendations and actions that have the potential for the most powerful movement forward. In the vignette on page 96, middle school teachers on Manhattan's lower East Side collect student data then reflect on it to

understand how to adjust their plans. After they adjust them, team members test further changes in their practice.

Promote learning, fidelity, and success

At each stage of the learning cycle, teams use a variety of tools and protocols to promote efficient and effective interactions. During the monitoring and assessment stage teams may also use several of the processes and tools that they used earlier in the cycle. Additional formative and summative assessments help team members check the impact of their work on student learning (see Tool 7.2: Using Assessments for Learning to promote conversation about using assessments to support student and educator learning).

IC maps provide direction

During the Learning and Implementation stages, teams may have developed and used IC maps. Like a road map, an IC map provides direction for getting from one point to another. It also provides a common structure and language for discussing and assessing progress. It promotes a shared vision and fidelity of actions for reaching it. When a learning team initiates a change, its members probably begin at a basic level of implementation with the intention of reaching higher levels of skill and proficiency in their practice. Teams use these maps as monitoring tools to identify their current state and provide direction for what's ahead and where they need to focus next.

Chapter 6 gives considerable attention to the value of this tool. The IC maps provide a common vision and language for discussing desired changes. Teams can also use the maps to support walk-throughs. Walk-throughs help administrators and teams of teachers gather information about instructional strengths and needs, monitor how professional learning is implemented, and measure professional learning's effect on classroom practices. The maps can be used to support feedback conversations from walk-throughs or support individual reflections. While they progress through the monitoring stage, teams may also use IC maps for data collection to support final reflections and inform future action.

Formative assessments inform student and educator learning

Formative assessments provide the day-to-day information educators need to gauge the impact of their learning and practice on their students. Formative assessments are used to monitor student learning to provide ongoing feedback that can be used by teachers to improve their teaching and by students to improve their learning. More specifically, formative assessments help students identify their strengths and weaknesses and target areas that need work … (Carnegie Mellon University, 2015, para 1).

Formative assessments help teachers assess their practice and identify where students are struggling so that they can tend to misunderstandings immediately (Carnegie Mellon University, 2015). As early as 1998 Paul Black and Dylan Wiliam (1998) reported that students who regularly participate in formative assessments achieve significantly better than students in matched control groups who experienced traditional teaching and assessment practices.

Formative assessments come in many forms and teachers have become more familiar and comfortable with using them. New technological tools also give teachers immediate access to formative data so they can adjust teaching in the moment rather than waiting until the end of a lesson or class period.

Ensuring alignment of formative assessments with curriculum units and modules is essential to supporting student growth. In cases when assessments are weak or misaligned, students and teachers do not have the benefit of identifying early challenges that can be addressed prior to summative measures.

During early stages of the learning cycles, it is essential that teachers check the alignment between the assessments and student goals. They have opportunities to do this when they complete the assessments and answer the question whether they believe successful completion of the lesson leads to success on the formative assessment. If they do not, they will need to determine if the problem is with the assessment or the lesson design. They can use the time during the learning or application process to refine where necessary.

During the monitoring stage teachers access results from formative assessments to determine if their lessons and practices are having their intended impact. Being thoughtful and deliberate about collecting, analyzing, and using the data is key to success in this stage of the cycle.

Summative assessments and adjustments solidify the learning

The main purpose of summative assessment "is to *evaluate student learning* at the end of an instructional unit by comparing it against some standard or benchmark. Summative assessments are often *high stakes,* resulting in a grade, reward, or consequence. Ultimately, the summative assessment will enable the team to make a decision whether students have satisfactorily met their goals for a lesson, unit, or grading period (Carnegie Mellon, 2015, para. 3).

In making adjustments to their learning agenda, team members may apply summative data to guide their decisions. Summative data are used in the initial data analysis and planning stage as a baseline for measuring success as well as pinpointing the

Learning cycle in London

While visiting a school in London, England, I observed a team of educators who were reviewing their monitoring and assessment data at the close of a unit of study. They discussed the observation data that was provided by a curriculum specialist and how it aligned with their original goals. They examined student work products and discussed whether they met the standards they set for the unit. They asked hard questions promoting deeper reflection about what they knew went well, where they struggled, and most importantly, what they would do with this lesson, and whether the students were ready to move forward — and how they knew whether the students were ready. They spent considerable time making notations on how to improve the lesson the next time around. Finally, after examining student work, they determined that the students had demonstrated sufficient mastery and they would move forward in the curriculum. Throughout the process they were brutally honest; they made a large number of changes to the lessons, and placed responsibility on themselves, not the students. And they noted a few areas to incorporate in the next big unit they would undertake.

— Stephanie Hirsh

highest needs. They also can provide information about students who need extra help and colleagues who have expertise to offer. In some cases, summative data can be used to provide rationale for repeating an entire teaching-and-learning cycle focused on particular outcomes or standards.

The team is near the end of a cycle when it secures its final summative data. At this point it has several critical areas that require attention. Most importantly, it will look to see whether enough students satisfactorily met the standards set for the unit or cycle. If not, it will need to determine how to adjust the learning cycle plan now and in the future. Near the end of the cycle, the team uses summative data to assess outcomes for students and educators. There are several critical areas that require attention. Most importantly, team members will look to see whether students achieved the goals set in Stage 2. If they did not, the team will need to determine how to adjust the learning cycle plan now and in the future. Team members will examine each stage of the cycle to determine areas for future improvement. They will also analyze student learning data to understand which students were successful and which were not. This data can inform not only future implementation of the particular unit or lesson addressed in the cycle but also upcoming units. As discussed in Chapter 4, teachers don't have the luxury of hitting pause on the school year or conducting a learning team cycle for each lesson. At this point, they will need to take what they have learned and apply it to help as many students as possible succeed, which may require particular interventions, assistance from peers, and adjustments to future instruction to emphasize concepts that proved to be a challenge to students.

Finally, if team members are satisfied with the outcomes, they may conduct a final review of any lessons they modified and assessments they used along with any assessments. With that review the learning teammates determine any improvements they want to consider when they reach this point in the curriculum in the future. The team may record notes, document assessment results, and indicate the strongest points of the lessons as well as the areas it would like to focus on in the future. Capturing this information now is important, because a year may pass before the team is again at the same place in the curriculum plan.

Taking action

Success at this stage is really determined by the work that led up to it. However, the ultimate success lies somewhere between collecting, analyzing, and reflecting on the data and choosing the next course of action. This stage, like those that came before, is iterative; however, at some point the team has to make the decision regarding its next moves.

In the London scenario the team is finalizing the monitoring stage of their cycle of learning. When observed, they were assessing and making final decisions regarding the quality of their teaching and the depth of student learning.

As the learning team members plan for and monitor the implementation, they may consider the following four steps:

1. Collect formative and summative data

From the very beginning of the learning cycle, the team knows that the ultimate measure of success will be in the final results achieved by their students. As early as the goal-setting stage, learning team members begin the process of identifying, studying, and developing the measures of assessment (e.g.coursework, projects,

or tests) that will be used formatively and summatively to demonstrate performance relative to their identified learning outcomes. The results may include an ultimate grade for student performance and insights on teacher practice and performance. Formative assessments for progress monitoring may include daily exit slips, observations, quizzes, student work, and weekly tests.

Summative assessments typically compare a student's achievement with standards. Common summative assessments are classroom tests, unit tests, benchmark exams, or external exams. Increasingly, teachers assign and accept project portfolios, product development, and demonstrations for summative assessments just as they would use student work and assignments for formative monitoring purposes. Teams may also review the data it reviewed in stage one to determine if there is additional data it wants to use in this final stage. All this data will be used to determine the level of success of this learning cycle.

2. Monitor progress toward goals

When team members regularly collect and use data about inputs, outputs, and outcomes of professional learning, they reinforce the value of continuous improvement because they are able to make ongoing adjustments in the learning process to increase results for students, educators themselves, and the systems in which they teach. If several teams or grade levels are working on similar goals, the teams may want to collaborate in the development of the monitoring plan.

During the monitoring stage, team members look for data about changes in teacher knowledge, skills, behaviors, attitudes, and aspirations (KASAB) associated with professional learning. They also collect data (e.g. IC maps, self-reports, and observations) to identify changes in classroom practices associated with professional learning. A team may want to

Teachers use data to adjust their practice and build student reading stamina

At the School for Global Leaders (SGL) middle school, teachers noticed that many of their students struggled when engaging in independent reading for more than a few minutes at a time. In the 2015–16 school year, the staff tackled low reading stamina by making a small change in English Language Arts (ELA) classrooms that they believed would lead to a big improvement in overall student literacy and learning outcomes.

During the teachers' weekly collaborative reflection meetings, the ELA team explored possible root causes of their students' struggles to read and identified student motivation as the factor that explained much of the variation in reading ability. They decided to create an incentive system during weekly independent reading time and study how it might motivate students to read more consistently.

The team conducted a small pilot study with three students in three different classrooms. Teachers taught students their expectations for strong independent readers and the prize they could win if they met those expectations. By focusing on a small sample, teachers were able to closely observe the students, reflect on what they saw, and refine the incentive system. For example, when they learned the early indicators of students needing support, such as turning pages too quickly, they shared approaches to getting students back on track. After four one-week cycles of testing changes and reflecting on the data during teacher team meetings, teachers saw improvement in the focus and reading stamina of two thirds of the pilot students. They decided to scale up the incentive system to the whole class.

When the teachers offered the incentive to the whole class, however, they saw less impact than before. This failure brought renewed urgency to their reflection meeting as they tried to understand this discrepancy. The team discussed what the formative data revealed about their initial theory. They paid special attention

School for Global Leaders at a Glance	
Founded	2008
Grades	6–8
Borough, District	Manhattan, 1
Neighborhood	Lower East Side
Total Students	235
Admission Policy	Limited unscreened
Co-located	Yes
Demographics:	
Asian	16%
Black	23%
Hispanic	57%
White	3%
Free or Reduced-Priced Lunch	79%
English Language Learners	14%
Special Education	33%
Attendance	92%

to the way they had communicated the expectations to the students and the adjustments they had made to support them when they struggled. They concluded that the incentives seemed to work only with individual attention and teacher follow-up — both elements that were absent from the whole-class adaptation. They revised their theory of change to reflect their new belief that individual encouragement and social accountability were more effective at motivating students than winning a prize.

With a new theory, they revised their approach: Instead of offering whole-class incentives, they focused on targeted interventions for individuals and small groups of students. As a result, the school is now piloting two types of targeted interventions based on individualized attention over time. By investing in this deliberate, data-driven process, the school built on existing teacher leadership and a collaborative culture to work toward their goal of making long-term gains in student literacy. The school predicts that their success in increasing reading stamina will lead to better outcomes on state ELA exams.

NYC Department of Education, New York, NY:

Samuel Milder,
manager of applied research

Natalie Pennington,
director of communications, knowledge sharing

develop, locate, or modify a framework to organize its efforts during this part of the cycle (see Figure 7.2). Teams may refer to Tool 7.3: Creating a Monitoring Plan for a resource they can use to develop a monitoring plan. Or, the team may want to display the data in the same way it did for the first stage of the learning cycle.

A plan is only useful if it is followed carefully. Creating a monitoring plan ensures that the team is able to collect the data it needs to make decisions about next steps. When they engage in ongoing data collection, analysis, and use, teams are able to provide stakeholders, such as school leaders, parents, or district staff, with information. Using and sharing data strategically helps sustain momentum and inform continuous improvement.

3. Analyze data and reflect on outcomes

During this step the learning team examines the data it has collected during all stages of the cycle. The questions the team will consider are the same questions it considered during the data analysis stage. However, in the data analysis stage, the team was determining its priorities to inform goal setting. In this stage, the team is checking on the degree of success experienced as a result of the learning and implementation stages.

The learning team may use some of the following questions to guide this work:

- Did students achieve the SMART learning goals?
- Did students in some subgroups achieve the goals while others did not?
- Were there any significant differences in the performance of student groups across classrooms?
- Did educators achieve their learning goals?
- Were educators more successful with some elements of the learning goal than others?
- Did all team members apply the new practices with fidelity?
- Where did members of the team struggle and where did they excel?
- What impact on attitudes and aspirations is evident?

Figure 7.2: Monitoring plan

LEARNING GOAL EXAMPLE	Problem solving for 6th graders		
Desired outcomes	**Indicators of success**	**Sources of data from formative assessments**	**Dates of analysis**
Educator Outcome #1: Teach two new problem-solving strategies.	Successful application of new strategies to teach problem solving.	• IC map documentation • Observation from peers • Student responses to two problem-solving tasks	Week 8
Student Outcome #1: Apply two strategies appropriately to solve problems.	Students select an appropriate strategy to solve problems. Students solve the problems with 85% accuracy.	• Computer-generated problem-solving challenges where students identify appropriate approach • Student work demonstrating appropriate application of strategy and outcomes	Week 9

- Are there implications of these data to consider in the final analysis?
- What data are missing to inform the next step?

4. Refine and determine next actions

Intentional action can be used as a phrase to characterize the work at every stage in the cycle. Taking time at each team meeting to reflect on learning and its application helps team members keep track of the essential learnings. With formative and summative data in hand, teams consider whether new classroom practices are helping them achieve their goals. They have at least three options to consider at this point. First, depending on the summative results team members determine that their cycle was successful and they are ready to initiate a new cycle with another round of data analysis and new goals.

Second, they may determine that their efforts resulted in success for some students but not all. At this point team members determine what they could do to address the needs of the smaller group so that those students meet the standards. Teams will be mindful not to create a tracking system, but to help those students who need extra support while moving everyone forward in the curriculum. This effort to address varying student needs could be the most challenging work team members face.

Finally, the team may discover that students in general did not meet the standards of performance. In that case team members may return to the learning cycle plan to identify adjustments and actions to inform the next cycle. They revisit their learning goals in Stage 2 and ask whether those were the right goals to address. Did their educator goals properly align? They revisit Stage 3 and 4 and ask, "Did we establish a relevant learning agenda and did we implement the new learning with fidelity and get sufficient support

in applying our learning in the classroom?" In the end, team members will record their reflections and use their analysis to plan the next cycle or address in the teaching of the next unit.

Regardless of the outcome, the team will document the results and the adjustments they intend to make (see Tool 7.4: Documenting Changes in Practice). Documenting learning and results is a valuable practice for informing future lessons as well as communicating with colleagues and stakeholders about their work. The team may also take time to conduct a separate reflection of their experiences throughout the entire five-stage learning cycle (see Tool 7.5: Reflecting on the Five-Stage Learning Team Cycle). They may find overlap among many of the questions, but a separate reflection will let them consider, document, and plan for non-instructional adjustments to the cycle, such as decision making or collective learning processes.

Reflections

- We commit to developing and using plans and tools to facilitate meaningful monitoring.

- We will be deliberate about integrating formal reflection time into each team convening.

- Our formative and summative assessments align with our curriculum and intended student learning goals.

- We can explain the difference between formative and summative assessments and the role of each in the learning cycle.

- We value the iterative process of the learning team cycle.

References

Black, P. & Wiliam, D. (1998). Inside the black box: Raising standards through classroom assessment. *Phi Delta Kappan,* 139–148.

Carnegie Mellon University (2015). What is the difference between formative and summative assessment? In the online chapter, *Whys and hows of assessment.* [Website]. Available at https://www.cmu.edu/teaching/assessment/basics/formative-summative.html

Chappuis, S. & Chappuis, J. (2007, December). The best value in formative assessment. *Informative Assessment, 65*(4), 14–19.

Clements, M. (2016). The importance of reflection in education. *Edunators: Helping Teachers Focus on Learning.* [Website]. Available at www.edunators.com/index.php/becoming-the-edunator/step-5-reflecting-for-learning/the-importance-of-reflection-in-education

York-Barr, J., Sommers, W.A., Ghere, G.S., & Montie, J. (2005). *Reflective practice to improve schools: An action guide for educators. Second edition.* Thousand Oaks, CA: Corwin Press.

Tools index for chapter 7

Tool	Title	Use
7.1	Learning to practice reflection	Use this tool to guide individual and team reflections in monitoring and throughout the learning cycle.
7.2	Using assessments for learning	Use this tool to support the application of formative and summative assessments and drive instructional improvements.
7.3	Creating a monitoring plan	Use this tool to help develop a monitoring plan.
7.4	Documenting changes in practice	Use this tool to guide thinking about how to document the impact of intentional learning.
7.5	Reflecting on the five-stage learning team cycle	Use this tool to reflect on the team experience throughout the five stages and guide adjustments to and documentation of the entire learning cycle.

PART III

How do you sustain continuous learning?

CHAPTER 8

Stay strong through the challenges

Where are we now?

We understand that change takes time and shifting our thinking and practice is a significant part of any change.

STRONGLY AGREE   AGREE   NO OPINION   DISAGREE   STRONGLY DISAGREE

We find ways to view the inevitable stumbling blocks as learning opportunities rather than barriers.

STRONGLY AGREE   AGREE   NO OPINION   DISAGREE   STRONGLY DISAGREE

We are able to recognize and build on small-scale indicators of progress.

STRONGLY AGREE   AGREE   NO OPINION   DISAGREE   STRONGLY DISAGREE

We take opportunities to remind one another of our purpose, focus, and larger goals in this work.

STRONGLY AGREE   AGREE   NO OPINION   DISAGREE   STRONGLY DISAGREE

We have strategies to jumpstart our work when we feel stuck.

STRONGLY AGREE   AGREE   NO OPINION   DISAGREE   STRONGLY DISAGREE

We are able to connect our challenges to our learning cycle plan and use them as opportunities to strengthen it.

STRONGLY AGREE   AGREE   NO OPINION   DISAGREE   STRONGLY DISAGREE

Overview

Teachers who are working hard to identify specific student learning challenges feel great pressure to improve their practice so that they may, ultimately, guide students in increasing their learning and academic performance. Teachers know too well that the students they serve today will be walking out of their classrooms in just a few months. They feel that if they don't help those students now, they lose the opportunity to do so. A sense of urgency motivates team members who are tackling transformation efforts at scales large and small.

This chapter reviews basic elements of the change process and about the learning cycle itself that contribute to a learning team's ability to sustain energy, focus, and momentum.

How do teams get back on track after progress stalls?

After a team moves past the exciting introductory stage — or enters a learning cycle for the third, fifth, or eighth iteration — they often slow down or feel hampered and may worry that they aren't making progress. Stalling within teams may look like this:

- A team has diligently worked through the five stages of the learning team cycle and spent hours in study, discussion, practice, implementation, and reflection. Yet they aren't meeting the student goals they so carefully set as part of the learning team cycle.

- A team seems to be treading over the same ground. They're tired of having the same conversations with their team members or getting to a certain point in discussion and not being able to move forward.

- A team is working well together and values their progress and process. However, they struggle to protect their hard-earned learning time, both from their own distractions and outside forces.

In any of these or similar scenarios, team members could lose motivation to continue. Once they do, they may struggle to maintain the focus and energy required to engage deeply in continuous improvement.

The good news — and the bad — about stalling is that it's normal, even predictable. And it happens to the most skillful and experienced teams. Plans rarely go as expected in schools, yet a high-performing learning team anticipates such times and prepares for them as do the colleagues and supervisors charged with supporting them. Having tools and resources to surmount challenges can be the key to team members' developing confidence, not only in their ability to implement the cycle as planned, but to expect and resolve problems that arise. Overcoming problems can be as rewarding as successfully completing a round of the cycle and celebrating student success.

Review change basics to overcome stalled progress

Many researchers have written about the change process in great depth, as discussed in "Chapter 6: Implementation." When facing a slowdown in progress, school and team leaders might review that chapter, especially the discussion of basic characteristics of change and selected diagnostic tools, to help them regroup, refocus, and return to action.

Appreciate the implementation dip

Chapter 6 also describes the phenomenon called the *implementation dip*. Team members may recall Michael Fullan's (2001) observation that "all successful schools experience implementation dips as they move forward" (p. 41) and realize they will benefit from understanding the implementation dip. As Fullan (2001) stated:

> Leaders who understand the implementation dip know that people are experiencing two kinds of problems when they are in the dip — the social-psychological fear of change and the lack of technical know-how or skills to make the change work. (p. 41)

This doesn't mean backing away from the work. Instead, Fullan suggested the following:

> … leaders who are sensitive to the implementation dip combine styles: they still have an urgent sense of moral purpose, they still measure success in terms of results, but they do things that are more likely to get the organization going and keep it going. (p. 41)

Use change management tools

As referenced earlier in this book, Shirley Hord and Gene Hall have written extensively about change in education. The framework Hord and Hall created, the Concerns-Based Adoption Model (CBAM) helps educators consider the beliefs and attitudes and readiness of learners to support learners in shifting practice. The CBAM contains several tools for supporting educators in change efforts. When addressing a slackened pace, the Levels of Use diagnostic tool, which was described in Chapter 6 (see p. 74), may be especially useful. Applying the CBAM model and this tool helps peers recognize that not every member of a team operates with the same knowledge base or skill set. When leaders and facilitators can align a team member's particular challenge with a stage in the change process, they may help the learner make pragmatic adjustments and, thus, accelerate the pace of the learning cycle.

Consider the theory about order of change when communicating success

Scoring small wins is critical to maintaining momentum. When learners can see that their efforts have an impact, they are motivated to continue. They see the value in putting time and energy into the learning cycle. Thomas Guskey (2002) proposed what he termed the *order of change*. In his framework, he suggests that teacher practices change first, and then student results, and finally teacher beliefs. According to Guskey's theory education leaders may invest significant energy in changing teacher beliefs to prepare them to make instructional shifts, but teachers are unlikely to shift their assumptions until they see how new practices affect student results.

For learning teams and leaders, this concept has several implications. First, team members will benefit from seeking a balance between investing energy in convincing every member of the team to believe 100% in every aspect of their work together and getting all members sufficiently on board to dig into the work. Second, building reflection throughout the process should help the team to recognize small wins along the way and assist them in moving through this order of change. Effective formative and summative assessments will provide information that may also motivate teams to act. When team members experience early wins, they strengthen their commitment to and belief in the cycle. As teams that achieve these wins, they may trumpet them both within and beyond their team. Building others' confidence in the impact of collaborative work is important for maintaining external support and resources. Team members may use Tool 8.1: Celebrating Early Wins to help get out the word about their work in progress.

Third, leaders of learning systems who regularly pause to recognize positive outcomes understand that taking time to establish rituals associated with celebrations is another way to confirm shared responsibility and accountability. Two examples developed by teams include awarding the "Golden Plunger" and the "ABCD Award." The first goes to the team member who took the biggest risk (plunged) for the team during the cycle and the second award may be given to the team member who went "above and beyond the call of duty" during a particular cycle.

Finally, communication is essential for two big reasons. First, decision makers who provide the resources (e.g. time, leadership, or external resources) to support a learning cycle need to know about team success stories for the times when they are faced with challenging questions. Second, the learning team cycle contributes to building collective intelligence and ownership for student success. After the team has identified what worked and why, it's important for team members to help spread and scale their most powerful lessons. Sharing information about the conditions under which the team is successful means more students may be successful.

Adjust for technical or adaptive change

Another key concept in understanding change is appreciating the difference between technical and adaptive change, which Ronald Heifetz (1994) highlighted in his work, *Leadership Without Easy Answers*. When educators are working on *technical* challenges, they use known strategies or call upon experts to help tackle them. When working on *adaptive* challenges, educators find themselves solving problems, inventing new solutions, and considering new beliefs. Heifetz makes clear that school leaders must lead differently to manage the ambiguity of adaptive change; moreover, learning and invention are necessary when organizations must break with old ways of doing things and stretch to accomplish new purposes. Not surprisingly, this process may be fraught with anxiety, fear, and

conflict. Heifetz uses the term adaptive to describe such challenges, and says that addressing them has an emotional component that often involves conflict. In a 2002 *JSD* interview Heifetz said:

> Conflict is essentially dangerous. That's why we are allergic to it. But conflict is a product of people holding different points of view about which they feel passionately. It's these differences that generate learning and innovation and adaptation. People learn by engaging with different points of view. Staying in the game with one another when we feel passionately about our differences is the saving grace of any community.... . In our effort to control the dangers of conflict we also eradicate the benefits of having different points of view within an organization. Conflict can be a resource that promotes creativity and learning. The orchestration of such learning is an important part of adaptive work. (p. 46)

Conflict, then, is to be celebrated rather than avoided. Indeed, conflict can be a sign that team members are confronting some of their most important issues and questioning their previous practices and beliefs. During these times they may find value in identifying and discussing assumptions as well as applying other strategies to manage conflict.

How do teams troubleshoot when progress is stalled?

In the learning cycle Stage 5: Monitor, assess, and adjust practice, a team examines the outcomes it has achieved and reflects on how its work throughout the cycle led to the results. When the team reflects on how to push further into future cycles or move beyond stumbling blocks, team members may want to dig more deeply into each stage of the cycle and consider what worked well, where they struggled, and what could improve.

In a check on team collaboration, team members can take the time to examine several elements of their work together.

Check whether the focus remains on the purpose

Working on one particular student and adult learning goal is certainly not team members' only priority. It can be easy to lose sight of the compelling driver behind the cycle, and without keeping that focus in mind, team members may lose motivation and energy for the work.

To move on: Team members remind one another about the student learning gap that led them to choose a particular goal. They consider implications of not addressing that gap and explore how solving that particular challenge will help them address other challenges using the knowledge and skills they are building.

Team members may also benefit from keeping visible artifacts of the cycle or other reminders of progress and goals. They also review where they are, where they've been, and where they're headed. This is a point where celebrating small wins is helpful.

Check for access to skilled facilitation and leadership

Productive team meetings require skilled facilitation. Team members ask themselves whether one or more of the members can play this role in ways that help the team move through the work meaningfully. If not, they realize that the team may spin its wheels during precious collaborative work time.

Team members may realize this is an issue when they see several signs: Not knowing what to do with their time together, not recognizing clearly the next steps needed to advance work, having unproductive conversations, realizing some team members are dominating while others are not engaged.

To move on: One or more team members may need to build skills in this area, whether through the support of a coach or the use of the many teaming resources available to educators. As with other challenges, the use of protocols can help teams meet productively, putting a frame on how and what the team will discuss and encouraging active engagement. Facilitation is one of several areas where a team should ask their coach or school leader for support to address the problem. Sometimes a coach may be available to act as the facilitator.

Check that team interaction has gelled

If a team hasn't had opportunities to work together in a substantive way, the members may be at such an early stage of development that they have difficulty diving deeply into the five stages of this work. Just because a group of individuals chooses to come together — or is assigned to do so — doesn't mean it automatically has the relationships essential to undertaking difficult problem solving. In psychologist Bruce Tuckman's (1965) classic article, "Development Sequence in Small Groups," he defined four stages of team development that many collaborative groups experience: forming, storming, norming, and performing. At the forming stage, everything is new, team members are polite, and don't know what to expect from one another. They are guarded in their interactions. As they get to know each other, they enter the storming stage, testing boundaries and authority, competing for power. Teams can get discouraged at this point; they haven't found their common ground. If they advance beyond storming to norming, they start to develop trust and are ready to get to work. They dive into the technical processes of collaboration. At the performing stage, teams have maturity in their interactions. They support one another and can be flexible and open in their collaborative work.

If team members become stuck, it is unlikely that they have advanced much beyond the storming or norming stage of team development, even if they've interacted collaboratively in the past.

To move on: One tactic for advancing team members' developmental stage is to intentionally explore this question together. Do they need to clarify their purpose, authority, and the roles and responsibilities of each member? Do they need to return to their vision and beliefs about the reasons for doing this work? Team members may also need to address or create norms for how they work together (see Tool 8.2: Establishing Team Norms to review and reframe how teams function during meetings).

Check that members are actively and equitably engaged

Some team members may come to believe that other members aren't fully participating and contributing to the team's work. Or, team members may find they don't share expectations about what they will contribute to the team. Such beliefs and experiences can lead to resentment that will harm trust and relationships within the team.

To move on: Team members need to consider whether they all have the knowledge and skills to collaborate effectively in team meetings. Perhaps the use of particular protocols can encourage all members to participate more equitably. They may also consider whether all team members have the content or pedagogical knowledge and skills to carry out the work

with students. Perhaps some need additional support beyond what the team can offer. As with the leadership challenge discussed previously, skilled facilitation may help a team function more productively and equitably.

Teams do encounter genuine dysfunction from time to time. Members may want to enlist support in developing clear roles and responsibilities of each team member during and between sessions (see Tool 8.3: Getting on Track to help reorient team members' commitments to the work). Team members must discuss how they will confront each other when a member fails to meet responsibilities. In addition, the team can discuss potential consequences for multiple lapses. Teams may be tempted to isolate or eliminate a "problem" team member, but they need to keep in mind that, if they do, the students of the team member will be the ones who suffer. If one or more members of the team are unable to resolve issues with their recalcitrant team member, they will probably need to seek the help of a mediator or someone with authority to address required changes.

Check that team members understand the cycle itself

Just as they used Stage 5: Monitor, assess, and adjust practice to look at the outcomes of the cycle, team members may now want to look at the implementation of the cycle itself. Do they have a sufficient understanding of each of the stages to carry out this work? Did they implement stages with fidelity? For example, in Stage 3, did team members spend sufficient time in the learning aspect of the work to gain new knowledge and skills? Did they choose a learning design that helped them learn what they believed they needed to know to achieve their learning goal?

To move on: The team might need help in understanding one or more aspects of the stages of the cycle. For example, maybe the district data guru could spend time with the team to dig further into the conclusions drawn from the data. Perhaps a coach within the school or district could play this role. Once again, the team may review its learning cycle plan and determine whether there were decisions that need to be reexamined and actions rewritten before they begin the next learning cycle.

Check that the team has sufficient allocated time

Even though the school leadership team has created a schedule that allows for weekly meetings (at least), team members may find that the time isn't enough. Perhaps they have failed to set goals at the right size to be addressed in the time they have. Or perhaps they find their work together to be valuable and they just need more opportunities to keep doing it (see Tool 8.4: Making the Most of Team Time for a resource to identify ways to improve use of time together).

Another challenge to protecting time allocated for a team's learning cycle work is the failure of others to respect that commitment. These external stakeholders may place demands on the team or individual members that require them to use some of their team learning time for other purposes. Team members themselves may become seduced by other opportunities in the building and allow themselves to be drawn from their shared work.

To move on: If a team simply finds it needs more time, members might consider asking their principal for assistance. He or she — or the leadership team — allocated the learning time for the team in the first place. Perhaps there is precedence for justifying more learning time. In this case, the team should be prepared to show how their team work is resulting in positive impact for themselves or for their students

and why it would be a worthwhile investment of more time.

The team members may need to get creative to find more time, or they may need to find ways to work virtually. Or perhaps they'll simply need to resize the scope of the work in the next learning cycle. In any case, the team should document and celebrate successes to maintain building- and district-level support for ongoing time investments.

If the team is distracted by other requests, it may need to revisit its initial beliefs and commitment to the work. If the work continually slips from the top of the team priority list, team members should explore why that is the case. Did they set the wrong goals? Do members not believe in their own ability to carry out and sustain the work? Do they not believe the work is important? How team members respond to each question necessitates a different course of action, whether it is seeking additional support, restating their vision to amplify the work's importance, or considering holding off on the work until it can take center stage again.

The principal can lend powerful support in resolving this challenge. He or she can wear the mantle of learning team champion in the contexts where that would be helpful by stepping in when other circumstances or educators try to rob the team of its learning time. As team champion he or she can also forcefully remind the team members themselves about the importance of this work.

Check to see whether the slowdown is within their control

Teams recognize that forces beyond the team's control can halt or sidetrack its work. Crises or tragedies in a school or community or in a team member's life will necessarily take priority for a while. Although such events put a hold on many day-to-day activities

Reflections

- We can identify problems that can stall the work of learning teams and have new ideas and strategies for addressing them.

- We understand elements of the change process and how it can impact learning implementation.

- We understand how making adaptive changes can result in conflict and have new thoughts on how to address it.

- We see the importance of identifying and celebrating small wins as a key part of maintaining momentum.

- We recognize that coaches and administrators can play key roles when teams are stuck; as a result, we have more clarity on the kinds of support we can request.

in schools, teachers may more easily return to the activities that are ingrained within their habits, schedules, and ways of getting work done than those things they consider to be "extras." Until school leaders have established a widely embraced learning culture that puts continuous learning at the heart of a school's work, a learning team's work will be a discrete task that can be put off until sometime in the future when it is convenient to begin again.

To move on: After giving sufficient time to acknowledge or address whatever tragedy, crisis, or interruption paused the work, team members may recognize the value and importance of returning to their normal routines. While it may take a few sessions to process the impact of a crisis, members may be able to use this experience to revisit the moral purpose of their work together. If the learning team work has been as rewarding as it's possible to be, then team members will decide that returning to work is an appropriate step to take.

References

Fullan, M. (2001). *Leading in a culture of change.* San Francisco, CA: Jossey-Bass.

Guskey, T.R. (2002). Professional development and teacher change, teachers and teaching. *Teachers and teaching: Theory and practice, 8*(3), 381–391, DOI: 10.1080/135406002100000512.

Hall, G. E. & Hord, S. M. (2015). *Implementing change: Patterns, principles and potholes* (4th ed.). Upper Saddle River, NJ: Pearson.

Heifetz, R. (1994). *Leadership without easy answers.* Cambridge, MA: Harvard University Press.

Sparks, D. (2002, Spring). Bringing the spirit of invention to leadership. Interview with Ronald Heifetz. *JSD, 23*(2), 44–46.

Tuckman, B. (1965). Developmental sequence in small groups. *Psychological Bulletin, 63,* 384–99.

Tools index for chapter 8

Tool	Title	Use
8.1	Celebrating early wins	Use this tool to review basics of change and adopt a strategy to celebrate successes and maintain momentum throughout a change process.
8.2	Establishing team norms	Use this tool to establish or review agreements about how the team will operate during team time.
8.3	Getting on track	Use the questions to take stock and consider solutions to create momentum when a team seems to be stalled.
8.4	Making the most of team time	Use this tool to assess team use of collaborative learning time and identify areas for improvement.

CHAPTER 9

Tie it all together

Where are we now?

Our school and district have an overall vision for excellent teaching and learning.

STRONGLY AGREE   AGREE   NO OPINION   DISAGREE   STRONGLY DISAGREE

Our school and district have structures and processes for identifying learning gaps and adopting learning goals.

STRONGLY AGREE   AGREE   NO OPINION   DISAGREE   STRONGLY DISAGREE

Our team knows how our student and educator learning goals connect to school and systemwide visions and goals.

STRONGLY AGREE   AGREE   NO OPINION   DISAGREE   STRONGLY DISAGREE

Our district provides all educators with high-quality curriculu and aligned instructional materials and assessments.

STRONGLY AGREE   AGREE   NO OPINION   DISAGREE   STRONGLY DISAGREE

As individuals, we know our individual growth goals contribute to team-, school-, and systemwide goals.

STRONGLY AGREE   AGREE   NO OPINION   DISAGREE   STRONGLY DISAGREE

Overview

The learning team cycle as described in this book was created to support teams of teachers working to improve student performance. While professional learning and critical initiatives may come from all directions in a school or district, prioritizing the essential work of teacher learning teams — and creating systems that recognize this work as essential — has the potential to serve as the vehicle for transforming student learning throughout a district. This is more likely to happen when the cycle is implemented with fidelity and has sustained support at every level of the system.

The purpose of this chapter is to explore how districts with a commitment to learning teams establish a coherent system that supports this high-leverage structure for improvement. Although coherence is ultimately a system-level responsibility, every educator within a system benefits from sharing an understanding of and contributing to the elements and conditions that make coherence possible.

What is coherence?

In a coherent system, all initiatives that make a direct impact on teachers are aligned and reinforce one another's effectiveness; from the teachers' perspectives, coherent initiatives are neither redundant nor contradictory. At the same time, to be coherent, all professional learning aligns with teacher, team, school, and system priorities. Such priorities align with the systemwide vision for teaching and learning and the instructional framework. When teachers work in a coherent system, they know their priorities and they know why those are priorities. Coherence ensures that teachers don't spend their time with professional learning that makes them wonder, "What does this have to do with me?" or "How is this going to help me work better with my students?" Coherence makes it possible for a teacher to recognize how team-based learning aligns with, and serves to achieve, the highest priorities of a school and system.

Coherence puts all educators on the same systemwide map, so to speak. Every teacher, every principal, knows where he or she is headed, who will travel with them, and who is driving the bus. They see options for getting where they are headed and they have the knowledge and skills to pick the most effective route. In outlining the importance of coherence, the Outcomes standard of Learning Forward's (2011) Standards for Professional Learning states:

> Outcomes: Professional learning that increases educator effectiveness and results for all students aligns its outcomes with educator performance and student curriculum standards. (p. 48)

The Outcomes standard encompasses three interrelated elements that professional learning must address to increase likelihood that it is linked to educator and student learning: meet performance standards, address learning outcomes, and build coherence. Of the last element, the standard further explains:

> Coherence requires that professional learning builds on what educators have already learned; focuses on learning outcomes and pedagogy aligned with national or local curriculum and assessments for educator and student learning; aligns with educator performance standards; and supports educators in developing sustained, ongoing professional communication with other educators who are engaged in similar changes in their practice. (Learning Forward, 2011, p. 50)

While the Outcomes standard emphasizes coherence of learning for any given educator, other standards also stress the importance of alignment among learners and across grade levels, departments, and buildings. In the Learning Communities standard, for example, alignment is a central element:

> Professional learning that occurs within learning communities provides an ongoing system of support for continuous improvement and implementation of school and systemwide initiatives. To avoid fragmentation among learning communities and to strengthen their contribution to school and system goals, public officials and school system leaders create policies that establish formal accountability for results along with the support needed to achieve results. To be effective, these policies and supports align with an explicit vision and goals for successful learning communities. Learning communities align their goals with those of the school and school system, engage in continuous professional learning, and hold all members collectively accountable for results. (Learning Forward, 2011, p. 26)

Michael Fullan and Joanne Quinn (2016) write about coherence in their recent book of the same name. Coherence, in their view, is a "shared depth of understanding about the purpose and nature of the work. Coherence, then, is what is in the minds and actions of people individually and especially collectively," (pp. 1–2). Educators create coherence as they make shared meaning about the work to which they are collectively committed.

Learning Forward's Redesign PD community of practice that engages representatives from 20 large urban school systems is tackling this problem and has defined it as such: How do we ensure that decisions made at the central office, school, and teacher level lead to both coherent and relevant learning for teachers that improves their practice? Teams may use

Tool 9.1: Creating a Common Vision and Tool 9.2 Agreeing on Criteria for High-Quality Professional Learning to create a vision of a successful and coherent education system with high-quality professional learning at its core.

Elements for coherence

Getting every educator on the same page in a district is unlikely to be a quick process. The structures, conditions, culture, and context of a system all contribute — or fail to contribute — to coherence. Yet without coherence, school leaders will experience variable success in changing practices and results, and they will be unlikely to sustain and scale the success they do manage to have (see Tool 9.3: Understanding the Elements of Coherence to check for coherence in schools and districts).

What elements make coherence possible?

1. Systems start with a **common vision for teaching and learning.** Such a vision indicates what and how students learn, including both student and educator performance expectations. College- and career-ready standards are included within this vision, as are professional learning standards. Since the common vision outlines what students need to know and be able to do, it consequently guides what teachers need to know and be able to do and is the basis not only for their professional learning but also teacher performance evaluation.

2. School and system leaders, with the ongoing engagement of teachers, **establish an instructional framework based on their vision for teaching and learning.** The framework includes an educative curriculum aligned to college- and career ready standards, and formative and summative assessments aligned with the curriculum. The framework establishes the district's priorities for

content and pedagogy. Regular examination of school and system data helps educators understand where they are succeeding and where they are challenged. They use those data along with their instructional framework to determine their areas of highest need and they identify student learning goals, educator learning goals, and ultimately an action plan for achieving both. Data from teacher effectiveness systems are one part of the goal-setting process, integrated into any plans for growth and improvement.

3. Leaders view job-embedded professional learning, grounded in Learning Forward's Standards for Professional Learning (2011), as **the most effective means for achieving their vision for teaching and learning** and implementing high-quality curriculum. The learning team, using a cycle of continuous improvement, is the primary means for achieving ambitious goals for students, and school and system leaders support, invest in, and protect this learning.

4. Systems create **strong linkages and coordination among central office departments.** The professional learning that many educators experience is disconnected so often because it comes from disparate departments that aren't communicating. If the human resources department is responsible for the teacher evaluation system, and the curriculum and instruction department offers professional support tied to content standards, it's no wonder that an individual teacher's learning experiences aren't connected. When departments work together to support and protect school-based teacher learning teams, teachers' potential to achieve their goals increases significantly. The Learning Forward Redesign PD Community of Practice members have referred to this problem as "silo-tude" and recognize the responsibility to

co-create that vision for instructional excellence and to determine each department's responsibility toward achieving it.

5. In a coherent system, there is a **clear, consistent process for introducing new initiatives and discontinuing or scaling existing ones.** Those educators with decision rights have a process to frequently examine whether initiatives are contributing to the common vision for good instruction, helping to advance progress for particular instructional priorities, or advancing teacher knowledge and skills tied to either of those. When school and system leaders agree that the work of learning teams is paramount, they weigh other uses of teacher time and energy accordingly as they make decisions about new initiatives. They also find ways to engage all relevant stakeholders in this process, circling back to the common vision as their North Star for knowing where they are headed and why.

How can educators remove barriers to coherence?

Striving for coherence makes sense. Why wouldn't educators at any level agree that all educators and all students should be working toward a shared vision for effective teaching and learning? Or that educators' learning should be tied to that vision explicitly, and that their learning moves their knowledge, skills, and practices to new levels of excellence? Yet, while educators may all agree, they might also point out that certain barriers impede efforts to achieve coherence: silos abound in a district or school; educators in districts and schools may lack knowledge, skills, and resources to build and sustain coherence; educators may lack a voice at the table for creating policies and practices that ensure coherence. Rather than view them as

In a coherent system:	In a noncoherent system:
Ultimately, any teacher's professional learning and growth opportunities offer the best demonstration of whether a system is coherent and aligned. Within a body of aligned learning, a teacher will understand:	If a teacher doesn't learn and work in an aligned system, he may experience something entirely different than his counterpart in a coherent system experiences. The teacher in a noncoherent system may find that:

In a coherent system:

- How her learning connects to the common vision for instruction and the district curriculum.

- How her learning at any given point connects to or builds on her other learning.

- How her learning connects to needs identified through her own evaluation as well as team and schoolwide goals.

- How her learning connects to or builds on the needs, learning, or expertise of her colleagues.

- Why she is in any given learning team, workshop, class, institute, or webinar.

- How those in a range of roles at various levels throughout her school and district support and influence her learning.

- Why her team, school, or district is taking on, or stopping, a particular initiative.

In a noncoherent system:

- The needs identified in his performance evaluation have nothing to do with the learning he experiences in his team or school.

- The school- and systemwide learning to which he has access fails to connect to his students' needs and challenges, and likewise, the challenges he faces in helping them learn.

- He doesn't really know whether his system has a vision that outlines what students should know and be able to do.

- He doesn't have access to a high-quality curriculum with which to align his learning.

- He is signing up for professional development options purely to check off an obligation outlined by policy or school mandate.

- He doesn't know what his learning team is supposed to do or why he is a member.

- He is uncertain about who in the district has responsibility for professional learning.

- He is unclear about where new initiatives come from or why they are happening.

immutable barriers, or "the way things are done," state and district leaders can view them as starting points from which to move toward coherence.

Eliminate silos that are common in districts and schools

School districts are full of well-intentioned educators working diligently to do their best for their students and colleagues. Consider, for example, the many ways that professional learning happens in a school district. Some learning may be controlled through human resources, while other opportunities may come from the technology department; still other learning may be facilitated at the school level by the instructional leadership team. Good intentions aside, such variety is a glaring indicator of how scattered any educator's learning may be. With their learning agendas, instructional frameworks, and communications plans, grade-level or subject-matter teams place a priority on implementing a high-quality curriculum and supporting that end. Though teams must also deal with competing priorities, they can use their planning to stage how they handle other priorities so they can stay focused on implementing curriculum and finding support to monitor and refine the implementation. In this way the teacher team integrates professional learning with high-quality curriculum and instructional materials.

From the district level through the individual learning team, one strategy for preventing silo-tude is sharing a vision of an overarching instructional framework or definition of teaching excellence — some districts call it their strategic plan. When educators know and understand what the plan means for them, they will be more likely to make choices that are coherent across individual, school, and system priorities. When the strategic plan includes

the teacher learning team as the most critical vehicle for increasing educators' capacity to implement high-quality curriculum, instruction, and assessments, all stakeholders across departments can align their support accordingly. A communications system, which is another strategy supporting the instructional framework, may reduce the silo effect by aligning and coordinating interactions among multiple offices.

Invest in the effort, skill, and resources required to create coherence

While many district leadership teams may take many of the steps previously described to build coherence, their efforts may fall short, and not through a lack of hard work. Creating an instructional framework, for example, is in itself a monumental process where educators at many levels come together to create shared language and shared vision. Ensuring that all educators throughout a system have the same shared understanding takes time and energy. Those responsible for creating coherence need knowledge and skills to lead such an effort. They need expertise in change management, system building, and communication and collaboration, along with a deep knowledge about student and educator performance expectations and effective professional learning.

Give individual educators or school-based teams a voice in guiding the direction of the system

Teachers address their highest priorities every day in their classrooms with their students, and depending on the day, they may find those priorities shifting dramatically. The leadership, culture, and conditions of the school and system in which they work will largely determine how connected those teachers are to one another and to any overriding vision for teaching and learning.

If the conditions in the school or district create expectations that teachers will contribute to ongoing plans for closing achievement gaps across the system, then achieving coherence is much more likely. By including teachers in planning and decision-making processes, school and district leaders benefit from teachers' suggestions about how to align district goals with school, classroom and individual goals and instructional plans. Teachers, in turn, have the responsibility to engage actively in such processes. When teachers are involved from the beginning, they play a key role in determining how to explain an initiative and may be able to get all teachers on board. The same is true for other participants who represent specific stakeholder groups in the process. In that way, communication, amplification, and staying true to goals and messages become additional critical components in ensuring coherence prevails.

What roles may educators play in developing coherence?

From the very start, teams of stakeholders, including a majority of teachers, will define excellence in teaching and the role and responsibility of each actor in the system to achieve it (see Tool 9.4: Defining Roles and Responsibilities that Contribute to Coherence). In Chapter 10, we explore more deeply how educators in a range of roles support the learning cycle and the system in which it operates.

Teachers

In a well-aligned system, teachers likely have many more opportunities to contribute to coherence. Yet even in a district that hasn't created ideal conditions for coherence, teachers can work to connect their learning vertically and horizontally and with that of their peers. For example, in a district with scattershot learning that has little or no explicit linkage to a guiding vision, any teacher can see the range of professional development variations herself and can take steps or make choices to link those options in ways that help her improve. She commits to the learning team to build her own capacity and to take responsibility for her peers' learning as well as sharing responsibility for all the students in her grade or subject area.

Instructional coaches and department heads

Teacher leaders with formal roles for school or team leadership likely have more opportunities than classroom teachers to see the connections between individual and team learning and bigger picture visions and needs. They can assume leadership for creating explicit linkages and seeking out learning for their colleagues that strengthens coherence. They prioritize supporting teacher learning teams and advocate to protect their time.

Principals

School leaders have a responsibility not only to understand the highest priority learning needs of the educators and students in their buildings, but also to create the conditions and secure resources so their teachers can meet those needs. A critical element is communicating clearly and consistently with central office leaders and other principals so that all educators across a system are working toward a shared vision. Like coaches they prioritize the support and protection of teacher learning teams.

Central office leaders

Educators who work in the central office are likely to have the greatest opportunity to create coherence within a school district along with the most authority to emphasize the primacy of the teacher learning team as a unit for change. With the participation of the system's highest-level leaders, they set the learning agenda, determine the budget, and guide the district's improvement plan. In addition to facilitating a districtwide vision, they are also likely responsible for many of the district's learning opportunities as well as the educator evaluation system.

References

Fullan, M., & Quinn, J. (2016). *Coherence: The right drivers in action for schools, districts, and systems.* Thousand Oaks: Corwin.

Garet, M., Ludwig, M., Yoon, K., Wayne, A., Birman, B., & Milanowski, A. (2011, April). *Making professional development more strategic: A conceptual model for district decisionmakers.* A working paper presented at the Annual Meeting of the American Educational Research Association, New Orleans, LA. Available at http://hub.mspnet.org/media/data/Working_Paper_on_Strategic_PD_Management_Prepared_for_AERA_2011_Presentation.pdf?media_000000008043.pdf

Learning Forward. (2011). *Standards for Professional Learning.* Oxford, OH: Author.

Reflections

• Our district's common vision provides the guidance all educators need to engage in learning that would best help our students.
• We have an instructional framework that serves as the foundation for coherence and alignment of all of our improvement efforts.
• We know who has decision rights for various decisions and the knowledge necessary to exercise them.
• All educators in our district share an understanding of the characteristics of high-quality curriculum and professional learning.
• We recognize the barriers we face in achieving coherence and possible strategies for overcoming them.
• Our team knows how to continue to build coherence in our learning and for our students.

Tools index for chapter 9

Tool	Title	Use
9.1	Creating a common vision	Use this tool to inspire the creation of a districtwide vision for an education system that is successful for all students.
9.2	Agreeing on criteria for high-quality professional learning	Use Learning Forward's Standards for Professional Learning and apply them to define what a system of professional learning should look like in a school or district.
9.3	Understanding the elements of coherence	Use this tool to understand and assess the elements that contribute to coherence in districts and schools.
9.4	Defining roles and responsibilities that contribute to coherence	Use this tool to build understanding of what systemwide coherence looks like and how educators' roles contribute to coherence.

CHAPTER 10

Advance the learning cycle with support of other educators

Where are we now?

Our school and system leaders support meaningful collaboration within a culture of continuous improvement.

STRONGLY AGREE   AGREE   NO OPINION   DISAGREE   STRONGLY DISAGREE

Our school and system leaders serve as model learners, prioritizing their own learning, often in collaboration with other leaders as well as teacher learning teams.

STRONGLY AGREE   AGREE   NO OPINION   DISAGREE   STRONGLY DISAGREE

Our school and system leaders provide structures and resources to support, share, and spread effective teaching and learning practices districtwide.

STRONGLY AGREE   AGREE   NO OPINION   DISAGREE   STRONGLY DISAGREE

Our school leader encourages leadership development at every level of the school.

STRONGLY AGREE   AGREE   NO OPINION   DISAGREE   STRONGLY DISAGREE

Our school leader recognizes and celebrates positive outcomes from learning teams.

STRONGLY AGREE   AGREE   NO OPINION   DISAGREE   STRONGLY DISAGREE

Overview

The primary audience of *Becoming a Learning Team* is teachers working on learning teams that operate within a school and a school system. Of course, their work takes place in a larger context, which in many ways determines what they can do and how they can operate. Because learning teams operate within existing structures, resources, and cultures, the work of the team is affected by other educators at all levels.

This chapter explores more deeply the roles of school and district leaders in making collaborative learning possible, more specifically the learning team cycle. The discussion outlines key actors external to the learning team who, nonetheless, make an impact on the team and its application of the learning cycle. Those external supportive others may also influence individual team members to exert their own agency and assume roles and responsibilities in mobilizing or leveraging system elements that support the decisions and actions of the learning teams. This chapter addresses those educators within the school system and outside who can bring influence, knowledge, and resources to bear on the progress of learning teams. Besides external partners, Chapter 10 also speaks to learning team members to help them understand the contexts in which leaders and other external partners can play roles that positively influence the progress of their learning cycle.

Who are the supportive others?

Central office administrators

District leaders have significant opportunities to influence the success of learning teams. If district administrators recognize their value, they are more likely to invest in their success. When they are highly invested, they ensure that teams have the resources and support they need to do their work and succeed with students. In discussing central office administrators, we encompass those in roles such as directors of academics and professional learning, assistant superintendents for curriculum and instruction or human capital management, and superintendents.

Principals

Principals' active support and ongoing engagement helps learning teams effectively implement or sustain the cycle of continuous improvement as described in these chapters. The principals in their schools have a critical role not only in providing time and resources for learning but also in creating a vision and culture in which ongoing collaborative educator development is part of a teacher's daily work.

External partners

Often, learning teams will be assisted by individuals who work outside the school system entirely. Those external partners include "individual consultants, organizations, agencies, companies, professional associations, institutions of higher education, or regional education agencies that provide services, goods, or products to state departments of education, school systems, or schools" (Killion, 2013, p. 5). External partners also can be tapped for expertise that does not reside within the team and is critical to its progress in the learning cycle. Principals and central office administrators play key roles in ensuring quality and expertise of these providers as well as providing learning teams with access to them. External partners have a responsibility to understand the particular challenge faced by a team and to assist the team in addressing it rather than take the team down a different path altogether.

With full recognition that leaders in these roles may have widely divergent responsibilities and levels of authority, this section explores how leaders' and external partners' actions specifically support the school-based learning team.

How do leaders and external partners advance learning cycles?

Create a learning system and culture

Principals' efforts to create a culture of learning are most successful within school systems that have established a systemwide vision for teaching and learning as well as the role that learning teams play in realizing that vision. They develop a strategic plan that makes their vision explicit and provide instructional coherence (Bottoms & Schmidt-Davis, 2010; Hull, 2012). Central office leaders use the Standards for Professional Learning to establish the foundation for learning teams. They connect student standards to teacher standards and use professional learning as the bridge to change practice so that all students have the kinds of learning experiences that help them succeed.

System and school leaders also are responsible for examining and adhering to the policies and regulations they create, and those they follow, whether at the state, provincial, or national level. They need to know how such policies, as well as any collective bargaining agreements, influence their learning visions and structures. They may need to take steps to shift policies where possible so that they support rather than hinder what they hope to achieve through learning teams. Their

ongoing relationships with teacher associations and state, provincial, and federal authorities are essential to aligning policies and regulations to systemwide visions for students.

Supportive central office leaders give principals autonomy to support learning teams. In light of a well-articulated vision from the central office, educators at every level hold professional learning to high expectations.

Although central office leaders are responsible for building a learning system, principals in turn may decide that their building will be a learning school. They are the leaders who can decide that their building will be a learning school — a place where everyone's learning is the heart of the work. Through their actions and statements, these learning principals continually express their expectations that all of the adults in the school take responsibility for every student in the school, and that they will learn what they need to learn to be able meet their needs effectively. Learning principals also talk about the importance of learning teams with all staff in their schools, with students, with community members, and with other administrators in the district. Parents who enter the building see indicators that professional learning drives the school, whether they see teachers meeting or artifacts from learning or calendars with team cycles delineated.

Skilled assistance providers take time to understand the vision, instructional framework, and goals of their clients including the school system, school, and individual teams. They ensure that they model the standards and other expectations in their work with learning teams. They seek feedback to ensure their efforts are viewed as helpful in meeting the specific goals and addressing the specific needs they are contracted to serve. They document their efforts as well as their impact.

Act as spokesperson and engage with the community

In a learning system, central office leaders create opportunities to amplify the successes that learning teams in schools across the district are achieving through their collaborative problem solving. They speak publicly at the school, system, and community level about specific team achievements. And they engage and support all leaders, including the school board, key staff, and influential stakeholders in sharing authentic messages. District spokespersons articulate the ways that team learning helps adults become better educators and how such learning benefits students. In such cultures, district and school leaders make the connection between their investments in professional learning and the outcomes that communities want for their children. At the system level, this might mean inviting a school subject-matter team, or even that same grade-level team, to speak at a school board meeting about their cycle of learning and how it improves practice and leads to positive student results (see Tool 10.2: Speaking up for Learning Team Work for a resource to help develop communications with stakeholders about learning teams).

At the school level, the principal and staff enjoy numerous ways to connect with the community. It might mean using the school's literacy night for parents as an opportunity to highlight a particular grade-level team's success addressing a particular student outcome. At any level, leaders can highlight team learning successes through social media, websites, or other community communications.

Model the attitudes and actions of a continuous learner

Learning Forward's Leadership standard emphasizes that leaders have a responsibility to engage deeply as learners themselves and to be public in their learning. This standard applies to every learner in a

---

Resources for finding time

Learning Forward has published numerous tools, articles, and resources about the challenge of creating enough time for professional learning. Start with the workbook *Establishing Time for Professional Learning* (Killion, 2013a), a full resource kit that outlines a comprehensive process for systematically examining and creating time use policies and structures that support continuous learning. The workbook includes sample schedules and is available to Learning Forward members at http://learningforward.org/login?ReturnURL=%2fdocs%2fdefault-source%2fcommoncore%2f establishing-time-for-professional-learning.pdf.

The National Center on Time and Learning (www.timeandlearning.org/) is dedicated to expanding and understanding time use in schools; find research, case studies, and models for time use.

Opportunity Culture (http://opportunityculture.org/reach/schedules/), an initiative of Public Impact, offers time use resources in support of empowering teachers in participating schools and systems.

system from district office to a school building. In the vignette on page 26, Superintendent Clara Howitt of Ontario (Canada) reflects on her experience as a learning leader (see "Letting a bright light burn — Leaders create conditions for learning"). Likewise, in *Becoming a Learning System* (2014, p. 58), Fort Wayne (Indiana) Superintendent Wendy Robinson paints a clear picture of the system leader as lead learner, "My role as superintendent is to be the district's chief learner and to model that." (Hirsh, Psencik, & Brown, 2014, p. 68). To act on that commitment to professional learning, Robinson established a district leadership team whose members would become a learning community that would lead by example (Psencik, Brown, Cain, Coleman, & Cummings, 2014, p. 12). Central office leaders benefit from such learning networks or teams that support their particular needs as leaders, building their capacity to play the very roles outlined in this chapter. Those teams will also benefit from using a team learning cycle to solve specific problems, though they will likely set goals using a different perspective than those explored in this book. The experience will not only help them to address shared problems of practice, it will provide valuable insight in understanding how to assist their teams when they have questions or confront barriers to the learning cycle process.

At the school level, principals, in their roles as instructional leaders, learn with teachers and teams while they focus on understanding and improving student learning in explicit ways. As instructional leaders, they might regularly engage in team learning to understand expectations and practices or deepen content knowledge in a particular subject matter. A principal who engages in continuous learning establishes credibility as lead learner while she develops the expertise required to provide useful feedback to teams and individuals. Principals also benefit from learning with others who serve in their roles as school leaders,

whether in districtwide teams or in networks that include leaders from outside their systems.

Improvement or external partners understand the learning cycle and its various stages. There are different ways in which they model their own commitment to it. They may discuss their experiences in their own learning teams. They may share insights from working with other teams applying similar cycles of improvement. They are respectful of the cycle and make connections to their area of expertise and where it fits. They assist learning team members to apply their new learning within the context and language of the cycle.

If principals and central office leaders have effectively fulfilled their responsibility of creating a learning school culture, engaging deeply as learners won't be a discrete task they undertake, but will be the underpinning of how their buildings operate for all educators, themselves included.

Ensure access to high-quality curriculum

A growing body of evidence highlights the power of high-quality curricula for student growth (Steiner, 2017; Chingos and Whitehurst, 2012; Boser, Chingos, & Straus, 2015). Those curricula can achieve their potential when teachers have daily job-embedded professional learning aligned with the curriculum they use with students (Taylor et al., 2015; Toon & Jensen, 2017; Wiener and Pimentel, 2017).

Districts have the responsibility to create a process for evaluating and selecting curriculum materials aligned with content standards. That process will outline the stakeholders involved in making decisions about curriculum along with protocols for review of materials. Districts help establish criteria for selection and allocate resources for the review process, purchase, and ongoing implementation of the materials. Districts also have the responsibility to establish expectations that the work of teacher learning teams will focus on the effective implementation of the curriculum.

Principals and school-based leadership teams are likely to participate in systemwide decisions about curriculum. They bear the burden at the implementation stage to prioritize teacher team learning on the selected materials. Principals will also need to focus their learning on the content and approach of the materials so that they can provide support as needed to teams.

Because coaches support teachers in the learning team cycle, they also have a responsibility to strengthen their capacity to use and understand the selected curriculum. They are also critical members of any materials selection and evaluation process, given their role in supporting teachers within grade and subject matter teams.

District or school leaders may enlist external partners at any point in the curriculum review and selection process. External partners may guide a materials review process or offer implementation expertise once a district selects a curriculum.

Provide resources

Central office leaders need to establish an organizational structure, process, and plan for the management and allocation of resources with input from a district planning team consisting of teachers and other school representatives (Garet, Ludwig, Yoon, Wayne, Birman, & Malinowski, 2010).

Principals, along with a leadership team, conceptualize a professional learning resources plan that outlines the money, materials, people, time, and other resources will be allocated and support learning teams. Depending on the district, the principal may turn to the central office because it is responsible for the coaching program, for example, and how that

particular resource is supported and allocated. They may also need to seek resources for technical assistance that may be available through various district offices.

Ask teachers what they need most for their professional learning, and often their answer is time for collaborative learning. Whether a principal is able to leverage resources such as time in her own building is determined by the vision, strategic plan, or policies of the district.

Countless considerations go into establishing a schedule, yet a principal who puts learning first will find or create hours in every school week so that all educators have opportunities for both individual and collaborative learning. After all, "a schedule is not what enables or disables collaborative professional learning. It is the top-down commitment to professional learning, or lack thereof, that promotes or hinders collaborative professional learning," says Jack Linton, assistant superintendent of Petal School District in Petal, Mississippi. He continues, "A schedule is a 'thing' that can be — and should be — manipulated in ways that are best for student learning. Collaborative professional learning does not begin with plans for a schedule change, but with commitment to a cultural change" (Killion, 2013a, p. 4). In many schools the principal undertakes this task in consultation with a school leadership team that includes teachers. Ideally, principals and school leadership teams will create schedules that make it possible for teams to meet two or three times a week (see the box, "Resources for Finding Time" on p. 122). Learning teams may examine their sense of how time is used in their schools with Tool 10.3: Examining Time Perceptions.

External partners or technical assistance providers, valuable resources themselves, can sometimes provide examples of how other schools and school systems are able to provide the time that teams so desperately seek. By their nature, external service providers may also save time for district or school leaders, thus allowing them to reallocate some of their time freed up by the output of contracted services or partnerships.

Provide access to multiple sources of data

Built into the learning team cycle is a step for analyzing multiple sources of data. Learning team members rely on principals and central office leaders to lead schools to give access to a the data they need most to make decisions and support them in analyzing them. District leaders can take several sure steps to help improve data use by teachers and principals, writes researcher Chrys Dougherty (2015). He groups the steps into four categories: clarify school system goals, create infrastructure for data use, ensure adequate educator knowledge on how to interpret and use data, and support collaboration among educators (p. 2). Those leaders will set and support the expectations that schools will use data to drive their decision making. Then, the district leaders will create an infrastructure for accessing and analyzing the data in meaningful ways, including identifying user needs, providing an electronic data system, and creating timely, user-friendly reports (Dougherty, 2015, p. 3). Whether there is a leader whose responsibility is to serve as the data expert for the district or whether educators at the school level take on that role, principals and system leaders provide support to teachers in getting to and using data.

Access to data is necessary for teams engaged in a learning cycle, but data in itself isn't sufficient. Making meaning from data is complex, and not every educator will have the skills to do so. Principals will need to find ways to build teacher capacity, and perhaps their own, in using data to drive goal setting and learning decisions. Coaches and system leaders can be helpful in this task, as long as they are clear about their

responsibilities in this step of the work and are skilled in providing support.

School leaders may contract with external partners to assist with this responsibility as well. The vignette on page 39, "Middle school-university partnership focuses on improving teacher data literacy to meet student needs" tells of a contractual relationship between Towson University and a Maryland school district that helps school learning teams use a six-step learning cycle to develop their data literacy skills.

Develop trust and relationships

Like allocations of time, trust is another resource that is embedded in the workings of the school and school system and has been shown to affect learning. Researchers have found that "while trust alone does not guarantee success, schools with little or no trust have almost no chance of improving" (Brewster & Railsback, 2003, p. 7). Central office staff and leadership set the expectation of trust — for the public and the professionals who serve the students of a district. In their policies, language, and actions district leaders create the conditions under which public and private trust grows.

Principals are central to creating an atmosphere of trust in a building, and this element is essential to effective team learning.

Anthony Bryk and Barbara Schneider's (2004) seminal research on relational trust in schools and its connection to student achievement established the importance of attending to trust and identified how principals and others contribute to the presence of trust. The way principals interact with other educators in the school matters: Do they listen to other viewpoints? Are they respectful toward their colleagues? Do they demonstrate integrity, carrying through on their commitments? Principals also contribute to an environment where teachers can be vulnerable and make mistakes as they work to improve, a result that is essential in a culture that values learning.

Strong facilitation from a trusted external partner has become a recognized strategy for improvement (Bottoms & Schmidt-Davis, 2010; Killion, 2013b). And trust, with transparency, responsiveness, collaborative engagement, frequent communication and constructive, honest feedback are attributes of successful relationships between external and district- or school-based partners (Killion, 2013b).

Assist teams in implementing learning cycles

Central office administrators are key to ensuring successful implementation of learning cycles. They provide the resources and establish the policies that determine the parameters under which learning teams operate. Central office administrators provide the curriculum, assessments, and protocols that drive learning team work. They monitor overall impact and intervene when system improvements are required. They offer support and expertise to school leaders who have limited capacity in their buildings to address specific issues that arise.

The school leader has the responsibility to assist teams throughout the year, ensuring alignment and coherence across teams and from grading period to grading period. He or she will have the bigger picture view that can help teams connect their work from cycle to cycle and stay motivated through the challenges they will inevitably face. During the implementation of the cycle, principals monitor how teams are functioning and intervene with resources and assistance as necessary. The principal might recognize when teams need to build their capacity to collaborate and offer support or find expertise in communication skills or addressing

conflict, for example. Or the principal may see that specific team members are creating problems; he or she may need to step in and intervene to help the team move along. While the team is monitoring whether its learning strategies are helping them to improve, the principal is also assessing teams' progress and offering both pressure and support as they continue striving to excel. The principal brings data, perspectives, opportunities to observe or conduct a walk-through, and other resources to the team that contribute to the monitoring and adjustment stage of the cycle (see Tool 10.4: Conducting a Learning Team Walk-Through for a resource to use in modeling or conducting a walk-through).

External partners provide particular support or interventions based on a team's need. If the primary purpose is team productivity, the external partner may tap a number of team-building tools and interventions. If the need is competency based, an external partner will more likely be working on building knowledge and skills and supporting classroom application.

Support leadership development

At every level of the system, educators need opportunities to increase their knowledge and skills in engaging with and leading learning teams. Principals, coaches, and teacher leaders responsible for facilitating learning teams need to know how to set norms and agendas, establish trust, communicate skillfully, and resolve conflict. District leaders have a particular responsibility for principal learning, and perhaps for coaches as well, particularly if management and development of the coaches is a central office responsibility. Superintendents and central office staff can support leadership development by offering teachers opportunities to participate in decision making and cross-district leadership teams. Whatever strategy they choose, system leaders who are eager to create a systemwide learning culture will find ways to bring teacher voices into every conversation about their learning and growth.

School leaders may need support to build their knowledge and skills in creating schoolwide learning cultures and structuring their time so they can focus meaningfully on their instructional leadership responsibilities. Coaches or teacher leaders may need to increase their facilitation capacity, content knowledge, skills, and data expertise so they can collaborate at the implementation stage. When coaches are in school buildings on either a full- or part-time basis, principals are responsible for collaborating closely with them to ensure they support teachers meaningfully, both as individual learners and members of learning teams. As Killion, Harrison, Bryan, and Clifton (2012) write in *Coaching Matters,* the "principal and coach work hand in hand to make quality instruction a top priority and create a culture of collaboration and inquiry," (p. 103).

Principals are largely responsible for ensuring learning for teachers and extending opportunities for leadership to teachers. When principals adopt a distributed leadership approach, then teachers have formal and informal roles, perhaps through leadership teams, in influencing their learning and that of their peers. Empowering learning teams with the responsibility and autonomy to work through the cycle described throughout this book is in itself an example of how principals recognize teachers as leaders, giving them the time and tasks to solve specific learning problems that can have an impact across schools and systems.

Principals and system leaders may engage with external partners to develop and carry out strategies that develop leadership and create opportunities to lead.

Use evaluation to support continuous growth

Research on principal evaluation points out that principals have direct influences on school conditions, teacher working conditions, and teacher quality, and indirect influences on instructional quality and student results (Clifford, Behrstock-Sherratt, & Fetters, 2012). Central office leaders support principal growth through their evaluation process. With an eye to shaping instructional leaders, principal supervisors use evaluation process to help principals develop knowledge and skills to improve teaching, learning, and student achievement. Supervisors may see that principals need particular help in supporting the school-based learning teams in their buildings and in recognizing that they have a responsibility to provide that support. They may also help school leaders see opportunities for growth within and beyond their learning teams.

For teacher evaluation systems, researcher Robert Marzano (2012) distinguishes between systems designed for measuring teachers and those designed for developing teachers. The likelihood is that systems do a little of both. While the principal has responsibilities connected to educator evaluation that go beyond how he or she supports the learning team, the principal can use information from the teacher evaluation process to help a teacher identify which learning needs can be addressed within the team learning cycle and which learning needs are best addressed through other means.

For new teachers or those struggling in their positions, the principal may see that intensive supports are necessary, and that even though the teacher is productively engaged in the learning team cycle, his or her needs exceed those of his peers. The principal and perhaps a coach is responsible for helping to identify and provide that support. For a teacher performing at an average level of proficiency, the principal can be helpful in identifying opportunities beyond the team

Role of coaches

School-based coaches have a particular role in school-based learning teams. At times, their responsibilities may overlap with those of principals, depending on the building and the district. They may participate occasionally as team learners. They may come in as experts to support a specific step of the work, whether in supporting data analysis or goal setting. They may facilitate a learning strategy, perhaps leading a book study or supporting the videotaping and discussion of a lesson. They might co-teach with team members or observe and offer feedback during practice sessions. They might help at the implementation phase, observing and offering input, following up with additional resources that support deeper learning.

Joellen Killion and Cindy Harrison (2006) outline 10 roles of the coach in *Taking the Lead: New Roles for Teachers and School-based Coaches,* many of which apply directly to how coaches can support learning teams in a cycle of inquiry. They describe the ways that coaches act as: resource providers, data coaches, curriculum specialists, instructional specialists, classroom supporters, mentors, learning facilitators, school leaders, catalysts for change, and learners (Killion & Harrison, 2006). There are times that learning teams will need support from a leader who can play almost every one of those roles, so ensuring coach support, where possible, will boost teams' ability to continue to grow through each cycle.

And finally, depending on the resources available to the school and the teacher leaders engaged in leading learning, coaches may act as full- or part-time facilitators of a learning team's time together. If teachers don't have the capacity to facilitate collaborative work, the coach may play that role. Or the coach may support others in doing so, stepping in on an as-needed basis at the request of the team or the principal.

to supplement learning to increase particular identified knowledge and skills. For those high performers who may be offering much expertise to the team, principals can be instrumental in finding ways to help the teachers stretch beyond their current capacities. This may mean working with the teachers to identify new leadership opportunities beyond the classroom or school or increasing their responsibilities related to the learning team or the school leadership team.

External partners, especially university-based educators or consortia of organizations, may play a role in advising on or developing measures or providing research-based information, other resources, and contacts with other state or district leaders who are designing or monitoring the implementation of educator evaluation systems. An external partner may work with a district- or school-based learning team to conduct the evaluation of the learning cycle and give the team evaluation data as well as assistance in analyzing and making meaning of the data. In Georgetown County (South Carolina) School District, the district forged a partnership with SEDL, a private nonprofit, to facilitate and evaluate their learning cycle. A 2011 *JSD* article tells how evaluation data first focused on tracking progress, but soon the SEDL team began using evaluation results to inform district leaders about how they might to support schools and teachers (Tobia, Chauvin, Lewis, & Hammel, 2011).

Reflections

- We can describe how school and central office leaders allocate resources to support the learning team.

- We know what role the principal and the central office leaders take in creating cultures and visions for continuous learning.

- We can envision a hiring process that supports a learning culture and various educators' role in it.

- We understand how a school leader uses the evaluation process to support individual and collaborative learning.

- We can identify various ways that technical assistance providers may be tapped to support the team and its learning cycle.

References

Boser, U., Chingos, M., & Straus, C., (2015). *The hidden value of curriculum reform.* Washington, D.C.: Center for American Progress. Available at https://www.americanprogress.org/issues/education-k-12/reports/2015/10/14/122810/the-hidden-value-of-curriculum-reform/

Bottoms, G. & Schmidt-Davis, J. (2010). *The three essentials: Improving schools requires district vision, district and state support, and principal leadership.* Southern Regional Education Board. Available at www.wallacefoundation.org/knowledge-center/school-leadership/district-policy-and-practice/Documents/Three-Essentials-to-Improving-Schools.pdf

Brewster, C. & Railsback, J. (2003). *Building trusting relationships for school improvement: Implications for principals and teachers.* By request series. Portland, OR: Northwest Regional Educational Laboratory. Available at http://educationnorthwest.org/sites/default/files/trust.pdf

Bryk, A. & Schneider, B. (2004). *Trust in schools: A core resource for improvement.* American Sociological Association's Rose Series in Sociology. Chicago, IL: Russell Sage Foundation.

Chait, R. (2010, March). *Removing chronically ineffective teachers: Barriers and opportunities.* Washington, DC: Center for American Progress.

Chingos, M. & Whitehurst, R.G. (2012). *Choosing blindly: Instructional materials, teacher effectiveness, and the Common Core.* Washington D.C.: Brookings Institution.

Clifford, M., Behrstock-Sherratt, E., & Fetters, J. (2012). *The ripple effect: A synthesis of research on principals influence to inform performance evaluation design.* Washington, DC: American Institutes for Research. Available at www.air.org/sites/default/files/downloads/report/1707_The_Ripple_Effect_d8_Online_0.pdf

Dougherty, C. (2015, April). *How school district leaders can support the use of data to improve teaching and learning.* Issue brief. Austin: TX: ACT. Available at www.act.org/content/dam/act/unsecured/documents/Use-of-Data.pdf

Garet, M., Ludwig, M., Yoon, K., Wayne, A., Birman, B., & Milanowski, A. (2011, April). *Making professional development more strategic: A conceptual model for district decisionmakers.* A working paper presented at the Annual Meeting of the American Educational Research Association, New Orleans, LA. Available at http://hub.mspnet.org/media/data/Working_Paper_on_Strategic_PD_Management_Prepared_for_AERA_2011_Presentation.pdf?media_000000008043.pdf

Hirsh, S., Psencik, K., & Brown, F. (2014). *Becoming a learning system.* Oxford, OH: Learning Forward.

Hull, J.C. (2012, April). *The principal perspective: Full report.* Washington, DC: Center for Public Education. Available at www.centerforpubliceducation.org/principal-perspective

Killion, J. (2013a). *Establishing time for professional learning.* Oxford, OH: Learning Forward. Available at https://learningforward.org/docs/default-source/commoncore/establishing-time-for-professional-learning.pdf?sfvrsn=6

Killion, J. (2013b). *Meet the promise of content standards: The role of third-party providers.* Oxford, OH: Learning Forward. Available at http://learningforward.org/docs/default-source/commoncore/the-role-of-third-party-providers.pdf

Killion, J. & Harrison, C. (2006). *Taking the lead: New roles for teachers and school-based coaches.* Oxford, OH: NSDC.

Killion, J., Harrison, C., Bryan, C., & Clifton, H. (2012). *Coaching matters.* Oxford, OH: Learning Forward.

Marzano, R. (2012, November). Teacher evaluation: What's fair? What's effective? *Educational Leadership, 70*(3), 14–19. Alexandria, VA: ASCD. Available at www.ascd.org/publications/educational-leadership/nov12/vol70/num03/The-Two-Purposes-of-Teacher-Evaluation.aspx

Psencik, K., Brown, F., Cain, L., Coleman, R., & Cummings, C. (2014, October). Champions of learning. District leaders build skills to boost educator practice. *JSD, 35*(5), 10–20. Available at http://learningforward.org/docs/default-source/jsd-october-2014/champions-of-learning.pdf

Steiner, D. (2017, March). *Curriculum research: What we know and where we need to go.* Washington, D.C.: StandardsWork.

Syed, S. (2014, October). Beyond buses, boilers, and books: Instructional support takes center stage of principal supervisors. *JSD, 35*(5), 46-49. Available at http://learningforward.org/docs/default-source/jsd-october-2014/champions-of-learning.pdf

Taylor, J.A., Getty S.R., Kowalski, S.M., Wilson, C.D., Carlson, J., & Van Scotter, P. (2015). An efficacy trial of research-based curriculum materials with curriculum-based professional development. *American Educational Research Journal, 52*(5), 984–1017.

Tobia, E., Chauvin, R., Lewis, D., & Hammel, P. (2011, February). The light bulb clicks on: Consultants help teachers, administrators, and coaches see the value of learning values. *JSD, 32*(1), 22–29. Available at http://learningforward.org/docs/jsd-february-2011/tobia321.pdf?sfvrsn=2

Toon, D. & Jensen, B. (2017). *Teaching our teachers: A better way, using K–12 curriculum to improve teacher preparation,* Melbourne, Australia: Learning First.

Tschannen-Moran, M. (2001). Collaboration and the need for trust. *Journal of Educational Administration, 39*(4), 308–331.

Wiener, R. & Pimentel, S. (2017). *Practice what you teach: Connecting curriculum and professional learning in schools.* Washington, DC: Aspen Institute.

Tools index for chapter 10

Tool	Title	Use
10.1	Supporting learning team work	Use this tool to encourage conversation among educators in different roles about how they support learning team cycle work.
10.2	Speaking up for learning team work	Use this tool to develop strong messages to share with all stakeholders about the value of professional learning teams.
10.3	Examining time perceptions	Use this tool to explore assumptions about time use and consider next actions.
10.4	Conducting a learning team walk-through	Use this checklist to support a school-based learning team in implementing the learning team cycle with structured feedback.

About the authors

Stephanie Hirsh is executive director of Learning Forward. Learning Forward is an international association of more than 12,000 educators committed to increasing student achievement through effective professional learning.

Hirsh presents, publishes, and consults on Learning Forward's behalf across North America. Her books include both editions of *Becoming a Learning System,* co-authored with Kay Psencik and Frederick Brown (Learning Forward, 2014); *A Playbook for Professional Learning: Putting the Standards Into Action,* co-authored with Shirley Hord (Learning Forward, 2012); and *The Learning Educator: A New Era for Professional Learning,* co-authored with Joellen Killion (NSDC, 2007). Hirsh writes a regular column for *The Learning Professional,* Learning Forward's bimonthly magazine. She also has written articles for *Educational Leadership, Phi Delta Kappan, The Record, The School Administrator, American School Board Journal, The High School Magazine,* and *Education Week.*

Hirsh serves on advisory boards for Learning First Alliance, Region IX (Arizona) Equity Assistance Center, Chalkboard (Oregon) Project CLASS Program; the University of Texas College of Education Advisory Council; and The Teaching Channel. She has been recognized by the Texas Staff Development Council with a Lifetime Achievement Award, and by the University of North Texas as a Distinguished Alumna.

Before joining Learning Forward, Hirsh completed 15 years of district- and school-based leadership. She has been married to Mike for more than 35 years. They have one son and a daughter who is an elementary school teacher.

Tracy Crow is director of communications for Learning Forward. In this position, Crow oversees the planning, creation, production, dissemination, and marketing of all Learning Forward products, including member newsletters, the magazine *The Learning Professional,* and books. Crow also contributes to the content development of the Learning Forward website and digital communications. She works with Learning Forward's leadership team to develop the messaging and marketing vehicles for products and services.

In previous positions, Crow wrote, edited, and produced a range of publications and products both print and online, including developing magazines, websites, and CD-ROM products for a federally funded project that disseminated information about curriculum materials to mathematics and science teachers. Crow earned her master's degree from The Ohio State University and her undergraduate degree from Northwestern University. She and her husband live in Columbus, Ohio.